THE
KEY
TO PAYING
FOR COLLEGE

UNLOCK SECRETS
THAT CAN SAVE YOU THOUSANDS

KEVIN SIMME
WITH DAVID ANDERSON

The Key To Paying For College: Unlock Secrets That Can Save You Thousands
© 2011 Kevin Simme and David Anderson

College Funding Alternatives, Inc.
186 Princeton-Hightstown Road
Building 4A, Second Floor
Princeton Junction, NJ 08550

Contents

A MESSAGE FROM KEVIN SIMME

This is a book of answers. There are lots of books to choose from that give lots of information but few answers about college financial aid. The book you hold in your hands describes actual case studies of what does and does not work.

What is key to paying for college? What is the key to getting good financial aid? The key is the process described in this book. The five main steps are:

1) **Pick colleges** that tend to give **the best financial packages**. (Chapter 2)

2) Do a **pre-planning analysis** to increase your eligibility for **FREE money.** (Chapter 3)

3) **Fill in financial aid forms correctly**, including the FAFSA, the CSS Profile and institutional forms. Read chapter 4 to avoid costly mistakes.

4) Once the college has sent a financial package, should you try to get a better one? **Learn when and how to negotiate for a better financial aid package.** (Chapter 5)

5) **Pay for college on a tax-favored basis**, leaving cash free for other goals. (Chapter 6)

This process will help you reach more solid financial ground. **With proper planning many families are in a better financial situation after paying for four years of college!**

My name is Kevin Simme and I'm a college financial aid consultant. Since 1997, I've used this process to guide hundreds of students and their families. The five-step process is always the same, but the choice of college and the payment plan varies. The choice of college depends on the student's goals. The payment plan depends on the family's situation. For example, how many children will be going to college? Does the family have a house? If so, how much of the house has been paid for? How close are the parents to retirement and how much have they saved? Are there grandparents who need to be cared for? All of a family's goals should be considered during the college financial aid process.

At the end of each chapter, I offer practical advice about what to do during each step of the process. Chapter 1 starts off by helping you understand the college financial aid industry. If you read only one part of this book, read Chapter 1. It will help you understand the strengths and limits of the people families often go to for advice—people like high school guidance counselors and college financial aid officers.

Read on and unlock the secrets that could save you thousands!

Kevin Simme

Chapter 1

Who Should You Go To for Advice?

Getting good advice about paying for college can be difficult. Let me tell you about the Warren family. The Warrens have a daughter named Jean who is in high school. They are doing the best that they can to plan for college. During her junior year, Jean's parents want to start selecting colleges and learn about the financial aid application process. They make an appointment to see their daughter's high school guidance counselor. The counselor recommends that their daughter apply to one or two reach colleges that might accept her, two or three colleges that would probably accept her, and one safety college that would almost definitely accept her. As for financial aid, they are told not to worry about that yet. They learn that the FAFSA, the most common form used to apply for financial aid, is not due until spring of the senior year.

Jean and her parents spend the junior year visiting and choosing colleges. During the senior year, she applies to one reach college, two target colleges, and one safety college. Her parents attend the high school's financial aid night, where they get a copy of the FAFSA. They learn that the FAFSA is used to determine the Family's Expected Contribution, which is the minimum amount of money that the family will be expected to pay toward college.

As the Warrens fill out the form, they find some of the questions to be unclear. For example, it is not clear whether they should include a non-qualified annuity on the form. They call the guidance counselor, who recommends that they call the Federal Student Aid Office—the branch of the U.S. Department of Education that administers the form. One call representative tells the Warrens that their annuity should not be included on the form. When they call back later with a follow-up question, they are told that their annuity should be included on the form.

The Warrens are confused. The Warrens call a college financial aid counselor, who tells them that the annuity should be included. At that point, the Warrens decide not to submit the FAFSA. They doubt that their family will qualify for financial aid.

In spring of her senior year, Jean gets her acceptance letters. As it turns out, she's been accepted to all of the schools where she applied. Unfortunately, the family did not understand the financial aid process completely. More importantly, they don't see how they could afford the amount they are expected to pay for ANY of the colleges. They call their accountant to discuss the situation. They also want to discuss whether they should use their home equity or their retirement savings to pay for Jean's college education. The accountant says that he does not feel qualified to give expert advice on such matters. He refers the Warrens to me.

Let me briefly list the mistakes made in the case of the Warrens:

- Jean and her family should have focused on applying to financial target colleges and financial safety colleges instead of following the guidance counselor's advice.

- The Warrens should have reallocated some of their savings by December of Jean's junior year to reduce their Expected Family Contribution. Don't wait until the senior year to do financial aid planning!

- If the Warrens had filled in the FAFSA properly, it is likely they would have qualified for need-based financial aid.

- If the Warrens had filled in the FAFSA, they would

have been in a better position to negotiate for better financial aid, even if they did not qualify for need-based aid.

- If the Warrens received the financial aid they deserved, they would be able to continue saving for retirement during Jean's college years instead of withdrawing retirement funds.

I wish I could say that these mistakes are rare. Unfortunately, they are quite common. For instance, a CNN survey found that 40% of families who would have qualified for need-based financial aid did not bother to fill out the forms!

In the end, I was able to help out the Warren family. I advised them on how to reallocate their assets to reduce their Expected Family Contribution. Since it was already too late to take advantage of the reallocation for Jean's freshman year, we did not apply for financial aid that year. To avoid drawing on her parent's retirement funds, Jean went to a community college during her first year. However, for her second year Jean applied for transfer to a new set of colleges. We chose four colleges that met two criteria. First, each college had a strong communications program, which is her major field of study. Second, each college tended to give students like Jean good financial aid packages. She was accepted at all of the colleges again, but with a major difference: each of the colleges offered substantially more financial aid! Jean's parents will be able to pay for her college education while still saving toward retirement.

So, who should you go to for advice on how to choose a college and pay for it? Well, of course, I believe that a college financial aid consultant would give you the best perspective. You may decide to get the assistance of a college financial aid consultant or you may decide to do it yourself. Either way, a family should have the guidance of someone with a solid understanding of the entire process.

The person you rely on for guidance should be able to answer these five basic questions:

1) *How do I pick schools that will give me the best financial aid package?*

2) *How can I lower my Expected Family Contribution and maximize my eligibility for financial aid?*

3) *When filling out the financial aid forms, such as FAFSA and CSS Profile, what common mistakes should I avoid?*

4) *Once colleges have made financial aid offers, when is it appropriate to negotiate for a better package? How do I negotiate?*

5) *How can I pay for college and still devote money to other important goals, like saving for retirement?*

This book is devoted to answering these five questions. Each question represents one step in the process of selecting the right college and paying for it. I have developed and refined this process in the course of guiding hundreds of families and individuals as a college financial aid consultant.

My job is fantastic! First of all, it's great helping people reach such an important goal—sending someone to college. But even more, I love helping people reach more solid financial ground. You may find this hard to believe, but with proper planning a family should be in a better financial situation after four years of college than before it began! Most people imagine the college years as times of financial hardship. That's far from the truth! I can help a family pick a college that fits their student's needs. Then I can show them how to pay for college and, in addition, pay for their house more quickly or have extra funds for retirement.

When planning for college, parents often look for advice from a variety of people. Experts, such as accountants and high school guidance counselors are typical choices, but parents also will consider the words of friends and family as truth. Each expert has specific training and interests that make them good resources for certain information, but which also limits them. It is important to understand their areas of expertise and their limitations. Friends and family may have opinions but are not likely to provide you with accurate, well-defined information.

In the following paragraphs, each expert has been given their own section so you can discover how they can be helpful to your situation or on the other hand how they can limit your success in this endeavor.

Accountant or Financial Planner?

Accountants and financial planners both have strengths. Accountants are trained to know the tax code. In terms of planning for college, they can be especially helpful in understanding how various college payment plans would increase or decrease tax payments. Financial planners are experts at making investments and providing insurance coverage. Financial planners usually offer families a variety of ways they can save money for college, along with the strengths and weaknesses of each saving plan.

Families who come to me after seeking advice from accountants and financial planners have told me about some of their weaknesses. Their most obvious weakness in terms of college planning is in the area of selecting colleges. Anyone going to an accountant or a financial planner will need to find other means for selecting the appropriate colleges that tend to give good financial aid packages. In addition, accountants are normally not familiar with financial forms like the FAFSA and the CSS Profile. What's more, accountants usually do not have time to help people with these forms. Their busiest time of the year is January through April, which is the same period of time when most families submit college financial aid forms.

Let me tell you about a family who called their accountant to determine what should be put on the FAFSA. The Birch family was doing the FAFSA themselves. Since they owned a business, the FAFSA was rather complex, and they were not sure what to put on the form as their income. The accountant advised the family to put down $60,000. When the Birch family came to see me, they brought the FAFSA and their latest tax return. After a quick review, I realized that they had made a significant mistake by entering $60,000 as their income, when they should have entered (-$104,000) due to losses on the business. This had an enormous impact on what the family was expected to pay for college. After correcting the mistake, their expected family payment for college dropped from $8,000 per year to $0 per year! We were able to amend the FAFSA and qualify them for nearly $5,000 in federal grants. In addition, we made an appeal to the college, which allowed the family to get the financial aid that they deserved.

Financial planners are generally biased toward savings plans, since it is their goal to encourage savings through their products. However, they will rarely tell you about the risk of saving too much in a college fund, such as a 529 plan. That's right, saving money in a 529 plan does have risks! First, any money put in a 529 plan increases the Expected Family Contribution—the amount of money a family is expected to pay for college education. Second, putting too much savings in a college account can prevent you from reaching other important goals. It is often better to use another savings option or to use a mix of savings options, depending on the family's circumstances.

I'd like to tell you a story that reveals a common problem that few accountants or financial planners know how to face. Mr. and Mrs. Santiago came to me to start saving for their son's college early. At the time they started saving, 529 accounts had not yet been created. The most common savings tool for people then was a Uniform Gift to Minors Account, also known as a UGMA or a custodial account. Basically, the idea was for parents to set up a bank account for their child and deposit money as a gift. As long as the child was a minor, the gifted money was not taxed as much as regular savings. The problem for people like the Santiagos is this: when the FAFSA is used to determine a family's Expected Family Contribution, the student's assets are weighed at a much higher percentage than the parents' assets. At that time, the federal government expected that 35% of a student's money would be used to pay for college, whereas only 5.6% of the parent's money was expected to pay for college. So, if the student had $10,000 in the bank, the Expected Family Contribution would go up by $3,500. If the parents had $10,000 in the bank, the contribution would go up by only $560. Since the Santiagos had been saving money in a UGMA for years, they had reduced their taxes. However, if they kept the money in the UGMA, they were going to drastically increase their Expected Family Contribution for college.

The Santiagos had heard that there was a new college savings tool called the 529 plan and gone to a financial planner. The financial planner was eager to help the Santiagos move all of their savings from the UGMA to a 529 plan. However, when the Santiagos came to me for assistance with the FAFSA, they were surprised to hear from me that the money in the 529 savings made their Expected Family Contribution higher than necessary. You see, the financial planner had transferred the money from the UGMA to a custodial 529 that was still in the son's name.

Although the financial planner had provided the family with a new savings plan, he had provided poor service: he earned a commission for moving the family's assets and did nothing to reduce the family's Expected Family Contribution. I was able to help the family by legally repositioning the assets to the parents' name. This reduced the Expected Family Contribution and made them eligible for thousands more dollars in financial aid.

When it comes to saving for college, parents need to be well informed and make good decisions. I follow two general principles when advising parents on a savings strategy. First, it is important for parents to save in ways that will not lock up their money and limit options for its future use. Second, parents should save in ways that count as little as possible against the family in the financial aid formula. A qualified financial aid consultant understands the impact of various savings options on the financial aid formula. The consultant will be able to present each savings option along with its benefits and risks and suggest a mix that is ideal for your family.

U.S. Department of Education

The Federal Student Aid office of the United States Department of Education administers the FAFSA. They are experts at filling out the FAFSA, the Free Application for Federal Student Aid. In fact, members of the U.S. Department of Education have been instrumental in helping me at times when I have had disagreements with colleges about whether certain family assets should be included on the FAFSA. For instance, I once helped a 17-year-old named Robert, who had recently been orphaned. His parents' assets had been placed in an annuity under his name. Robert came to me when the college he was attending had withdrawn their initial offer of financial aid, stating that the annuity should be used to cover his college costs. When I told the college that the annuity should not have been included on the FAFSA, the college disagreed. At that point, I discussed the situation with a senior administrator at the U.S. Department of Education, who confirmed that the annuity should not be included on the FAFSA and agreed to discuss the situation with the college. The FAFSA senior administrator helped me resolve the matter and the college was forced to reinstate Robert's initial offer of financial aid. What a relief!

I am grateful to the Department of Education for their assistance to Robert and for their help in other situations. Still, I have to acknowledge that the office of Federal Student Aid has some weaknesses. Parents have come to me for help because they have received conflicting information from the office. Parents have spoken to a phone representative and received an answer to a question, then called later for additional details, only to receive conflicting information from another phone representative. How frustrating! Yet the Department of Education printed the following message on their 2011 publication, "Funding Education Beyond High School":

REMEMBER, you can get all the help you need for **FREE** from one of these sources. **NEVER** pay anyone for assistance in completing the online or paper FAFSA.

I find it odd that the Department of Education has this notice printed on the FAFSA. Why should people be warned against paying someone for assistance? The FAFSA has questions about income that are as vague and frustrating as questions on income tax forms. Why doesn't the U.S. Department of the Treasury put a notice on Form 1040 that people should not pay accountants or tax advisors to fill out their tax forms? After all, you can get free help from the Internal Revenue Service, right? Even if such a notice were on Form 1040, would that stop you from paying someone for assistance?

It is difficult to get consistent, reliable advice from the office of Federal Student Aid. But an even more important problem is this: it is not their business to help you reposition funds to reduce your Expected Family Contribution. Let me illustrate with an example. Mrs. Khan came to me with her daughter Monica, who was getting ready to apply to college. The father had passed away years earlier in a car accident and money had been awarded to Monica in a custodial account as part of a court settlement. When the mother called the office of Federal Student Aid about whether the asset was hers or her daughters, the office simply responded that the asset was her daughters. That's how the office works. When asked how to classify any asset, the representative will respond by saying it's either the parent's asset or the student's asset. It's not the office's responsibility to advise callers that there are legal ways of repositioning student assets to minimize the Expected Family Contribution. In my position as their college financial aid consultant, I advised Mrs. Khan and her daughter to reposition the money from the custodial account into another savings plan so that the money did not count as a student asset. As a result, we reduced their Expected Family Contribution by thousands of dollars.

It is not the job of the office of Federal Student Aid to give advice on reallocating assets. Their job is to inform people of the rules and regulations regarding current assets. Nor is it the office's job to help you negotiate a better financial aid package. The list could go on, but my point is clear: the office of Federal Student Aid is not in the business of helping you finance a college education effectively. On the other hand, as a college financial aid consultant, it's my job to help you find ways to minimize your Expected Family Contribution, to get the best financial aid package, and to pay for college in the most tax-advantaged way. On top of that, I will do all this as one step in the process toward helping your family achieve its financial goals.

Oh, and by the way, colleges often require families to fill in other financial aid forms—the CSS Profile or the college's own financial aid form. The office of Federal Student Aid certainly won't help you with those forms. So how about getting help from a financial aid officer at the college?

College Financial Aid Officers

I have many good things to say about college financial aid officers. In my experience, each college has at least one person in the office who understands financial aid rules and regulations thoroughly. In addition, many college financial aid officers have a desire to serve their college and its students. However, I would not seek assistance from a college financial aid officer to help me do my financial aid planning.

The main goal of a financial aid officer is to attract as many students as possible with as little institutional financial aid as possible. Look at things from the perspective of a financial aid officer: there is a certain amount of money available and a certain number of spaces available—let's say 1,000 spaces for freshmen. The institution wants to attract highly qualified students—the ones with good grades, high class ranks, and high test scores. The institution may accept and make financial aid offers to about 3,000 students. Highly qualified students typically get better offers than those with lower grades and scores. Now, the financial aid offers had better not be too good, or else all 3,000 offers would be accepted. That would create a huge mess: there would be overcrowding, plus the college would probably have a hard time paying all the money that was offered. So, the object of the financial officer's game is to offer enough money to lure the right number of students within the given budget.

Is this person going to tell you that the annuity from your inheritance does not belong on the FAFSA? No, that certainly didn't happen in Robert's situation. Is this person going to help you allocate your assets to reduce your Expected Family Contribution? No! Will this person help you negotiate a better financial aid package? NO WAY!

Now please don't get me wrong: every institution needs financial aid officers. It's an essential job. In fact, I encourage you to meet a college financial aid officer when you go on a campus visit. The officer will let you know which forms the institution requires and inform you of important deadlines. You will also learn about scholarship opportunities available for your student at that college. Still, you should not go to the financial aid officer for advice on allocating your assets, filling in financial aid forms, or creating a payment plan. These are better left to a college financial aid consultant who has your family's goals in mind.

High School Guidance Counselor

At their best, high school guidance counselors can help you with the admissions process. They are often good at helping students select appropriate courses and encouraging involvement in the right activities to become attractive college applicants. Students also rely on guidance counselors for transcripts, letters of recommendation, and advice for filling in college applications. In addition, guidance counselors can often recommend colleges that have strong programs in line with your student's interests, whether it's becoming an English teacher or an engineer. In my experience, the problem with relying on a high school guidance counselor is this: they often help students choose colleges without considering the family's financial situation. To illustrate this, I recall attending a financial aid workshop as a parent and the director of the local high school guidance department asked me to sit down in the front and take good notes because members of the guidance department "were not familiar with any of this stuff." The members of the high school guidance office rely heavily on the college financial aid officers for information. That's why financial aid night at a high school typically features presentations given by college financial aid officers. On top of that, high school guidance counselors often have too many students to help, preventing them from giving the best guidance available.

Let me tell you a true story about a young woman named Lynn. When Lynn entered high school, she had her heart set on going to college to become a science teacher. She told her guidance counselor Mr. Miller about her intentions in her sophomore year. She did everything Mr. Miller told her to do. She took the most difficult science and math courses that she could, including an advanced biology course and pre-calculus. She studied hard, making the honor roll every term with more A's than B's. In her senior year, she was ranked in the top 25% of her class and she earned a high SAT score. Mr. Miller knew of a nearby private university with an excellent teacher education program. The school was prestigious and highly selective, but Mr. Miller believed that Lynn had the courses, grades, and SAT scores that she needed to get in. Lynn visited the university and thought it was the ideal place. She visited a few state colleges as well, but she was determined to get into the prestigious, private university. On the advice of her guidance counselor, Lynn applied to the university under their early decision program. If she were accepted, she would be under contract to attend the university, but Mr. Miller told Lynn that she had nothing to lose. If she were accepted, her greatest dream would come true. And, if she were not accepted, she would still have time to apply to other schools.

Six weeks after applying to the university, Lynn was overjoyed to receive an acceptance letter. Her parents were thrilled. Lynn showed the letter to Mr. Miller the next day, gushing with thanks and appreciation. It seemed as if Lynn's dream had come true and she would get the college education and career she had always wanted.

Lynn's dream began to unfold several months later when the college sent her their financial aid offer. Based on Lynn's difficult courses, good grades, and high SAT score, the college awarded her with a merit scholarship that covered one third of the tuition. Based on the family's income, she received grants and work study aid, which, together with the scholarship, would cover about half of the cost of attendance (tuition, fees, room, board, books, supplies, and living expenses) —a total of about $40,000 per year. The problem was that Lynn and her family would be expected to pay the other half of the total cost. Over the course of four years, the family's payment would come to a total of over $80,000. Lynn's parents did not think they were in a position to pay this amount of money. They had to ask their daughter if she would settle for one of the state colleges with more affordable costs. After gaining acceptance to the private university of her dreams, Lynn was reluctant to accept the idea of going to a state college, but that would be better than nothing. With a heavy heart, she went to Mr. Miller to tell her that she would need to send applications to the state colleges even though she had been accepted at the university.

The problems had only begun. Mr. Miller was surprised to hear the news. He was also concerned because he knew that acceptance by early decision meant that Lynn could not be accepted at other colleges. Even if Lynn managed to break the contract with the private university, other colleges were not likely to accept a student who had broken such a contract at such a late date. Mr. Miller explained to Lynn that she would not be able to apply to other colleges because of her acceptance through the early decision program.

By the time Lynn reached my office, there was little that could be done. The prestigious university had many applicants that were even more qualified than she was, and the financial aid office was unwilling to increase her package. She had only two options left. First, she could go to a community college. Second, she could stay home for a year. In the end, she decided to attend community college until she could gain admission into another college.

I was glad that Lynn was at least able to attend a college and keep her dream of becoming a science teacher alive. Still, this is a clear illustration of a point: high school guidance counselors often lack the time or the knowledge of the financial aid system to help a student choose colleges that meet the family's financial profile. In Lynn's case, if she had come to me earlier, I could have helped her a great deal. It was a shame that she was advised to apply to a prestigious university that, in the end, was not affordable. Why apply to a college if you can't pay for it? Applying for early decision made the situation even more tragic. Given what I learned about her family's financial situation and goals, I have advised her to apply to several private colleges that tend to offer very good financial aid to attract students of her high caliber. Although these colleges may not be as prestigious as the university where she was first accepted, they each offer a high quality education that will help her achieve her goal of becoming a science teacher. I will be gratified to see her enter one of these colleges as a sophomore. I wish I could have helped her enter as a freshman.

Mr. Miller helped Lynn the best that he could. He helped her get enrolled in the right types of classes and told her what she needed to do to get accepted to a good university. He helped her find a college that had a great program in her area of interest and get her application materials in on time. With his help she was accepted. However, without knowing the family's financial situation, that help was not enough to get Lynn into the college of her choice.

Lynn happened to go to a public high school, but students who go to private high schools are not immune from this problem. I have helped a number of families who were not served well by college counselors at private schools. For instance, I recently worked with a young man named Jim Gilmore and his family. Jim was born in a city and began going to a city high school that had a reputation for gang violence. Jim was a good student and his mother wanted him to get a better education. She managed to get him admitted to a prestigious college prep school, which she paid for with the help of financial aid. Jim thrived at the private high school, earning good grades and a high SAT score. However, when the time came for Jim to apply to colleges, the college counselor did not take into account the family's financial situation. You see, private high schools have a vested interest in getting their students into the most prestigious schools possible. Many parents choose private high schools based on their success at getting their students into prestigious colleges, and private schools gain good reputations for their success at this. When the college counselor helped Jim select colleges, the counselor assumed that Jim would want to apply to the most prestigious colleges where he could gain admission. Jim was accepted at many of the colleges where he applied. The college that provided the best financial aid offer required the family to pay $8,000 per year. The family's resources had already been stretched to the limit when paying for the private high school. There was no way that the family would be able to pay or borrow $32,000 for four years of college. Jim's father had no contact with the family for many years, and his mom was on welfare at this point. The family was renting, so they had no equity to draw on. This was an obvious situation that the guidance counselor should have taken into consideration. However, the college counselor failed to become familiar with the family's financial situation, and he advised Jim to apply to colleges that did not offer enough financial aid. By the time Jim came to me, it was too late. He had to attend community college and wait to transfer to a four-year college. As with Lynn, I am helping Jim select colleges that have quality programs and that tend to offer very good financial aid to students like Jim.

One common problem is for guidance counselors to recommend colleges that do not tend to offer good financial aid. Another common problem is that guidance counselors often think of state colleges and community colleges as the only low-cost colleges. Students sometimes tell their guidance counselor that the family has little money to pay for college. Without thorough knowledge of the financial aid system, guidance counselors often advise such students to apply to large state schools or the local community college. I wish I could speak to every family who hears this poor advice! What guidance counselors don't know is that many students could get a more affordable education at a private college. On top of that, the private colleges that I recommend often offer a better education than the typical state college. Why should you pay more for large classes taught by graduate assistants? If you know which colleges tend to offer good financial aid, you will pay less for smaller classes that are taught by passionate, full-time professors.

Whatever your financial situation might be, it is important for you to get the greatest value for your dollar. A qualified college financial aid consultant will guide you through the financial aid process along with the application process. The two processes go hand in hand. The family's financial profile, along with the student's interests, should guide the choice of schools. The college should fit the student's educational needs and the family's financial goals.

Loan Companies

Once financial aid offers come, the first thing many families do is start shopping around for loans. They'll seek out loan companies to find the best rates and see how much they can borrow. Loan companies are important because they provide products that allow students to attend college. Without them, families would not be able to make the investment needed to pay for four years of college education. Still, you need to understand the extent to which a loan officer can help you. The goal of the loan officer is to provide you with the largest loan that you can qualify for. A loan officer is not going to help you find a way to pay for four years of education in an efficient way. Let me provide an example of two families—the Meyers and the Stallones.

Imagine that the housing market is great and interest rates are low. Both the Meyers and the Stallones plan to use the equity in their homes to pay for four years of college, but several aspects of their plan vary considerably. Let's look at the Meyers' plan first. The Meyers don't do planning to minimize college costs. They don't pick colleges that tend to provide good financial aid and they don't try to allocate resources to minimize their Expected Family Contribution. In fact, they doubt that they'll get any financial aid, so they don't bother filling in the FAFSA. They know that they have $120,000 of equity in their home and their college will cost about $30,000 per year. Their attitude is, "We can afford it." Their plan is to go to a loan company, open up a $120,000 line of credit on their home, and write a check for college costs each semester. Everything goes as planned during the first two years: the student goes to college and the Meyers use $60,000 in equity on their home. Unexpected problems arrive in the second year. The housing market falls and so does the value of the house. The loan company needs to ensure that they don't lend out more money than the house is worth, so they decide to close the Meyers' line of credit. What can the Meyers do? Well, they've got to find alternate ways of funding their student's college education. I would recommend that they reallocate their assets and apply for financial aid. In fact, that's what they should have done from the beginning! On top of that, I would recommend a better payment plan.

Now let's look at the Stallone family. The Stallones have $120,000 of equity in their home that they plan to leverage as well. However, they want to preserve as much of that equity as possible. They reposition their equity, apply to colleges that tend to give good financial aid, and go through the financial aid process. As it turns out, they don't qualify for need-based aid, but the colleges to which the student applied tend to offer good merit scholarships. In the end, the college they choose costs $34,000 per year, but merit scholarships reduce their out of pocket costs to only $15,000 per year. By doing proper planning, the Stallones will pay $60,000 less than the Meyers for four years of college.

The Stallones have already gained one major financial advantage over the Meyers. The Stallones can gain an even further advantage by using a payment plan that actually reduces the length of their mortgage. When their student begins college, the family has 18 years left on the mortgage. I would recommend a payment plan that would use their equity to pay for college. In addition, the plan would allow them to pay off their mortgage in about 14 years instead of 18 years! A loan officer would not be in a position to recommend such a payment plan because it involves financing that is not offered by a loan company. Let me describe how the payment plan works. Instead of borrowing $15,000 each year to pay for college, they refinance their mortgage and borrow the whole $60,000 at once. The Stallones pay $7,500 for the first semester of college and place the remaining $52,500 in a secure savings vehicle that has minimum guarantees and that is not open to stock market risk. Their mortgage is now extended to 30 years with a higher principal amount. However, over the next four years, the Stallones use the secure savings vehicle to pay for college. Earnings from the savings vehicle allow the fund to continue even after their student graduates. The Stallones let the remaining fund grow until it becomes large enough to let them pay off their mortgage. Instead of taking 18 years to finish paying the mortgage, they can pay it off in 14 years if they choose. They could also use the earnings for a variety of other purposes, such as retirement, travel, or a vacation home.

Your family's payment plan may be very different from the Stallones' plan. Maybe you have a house, but you don't have enough equity to cover college costs. Or maybe you don't own a house, but you have some college savings. Your family's payment plan depends on your family's financial situation and financial goals. Loans are just one option within an overall payment plan. Your family needs to devise a reasonable, long-term payment plan before going to a loan company. A loan company will let you borrow whatever you can, which is not an effective plan. Before you even think about calling a loan company, it's important to go through two stages of financial aid planning with a knowledgeable consultant.

The first type of planning is the pre-planning analysis, which I discuss in more detail in Chapter 3. The pre-planning analysis helps you decide on your family's goals and allocate finances accordingly. With proper asset allocation, you will qualify for the maximum amount of free money. By free money, I mean grants and scholarships that you won't repay. Pre-planning allows you to get more free money and borrow less money! Pre-planning and asset allocation both need to be completed before the financial aid applications are submitted—long before loan companies enter the picture.

The second stage of planning is the how-to-pay plan, which

I write about in Chapter 6. At this stage, your family has already chosen a college. If it's appropriate, your family should have negotiated an even better financial aid package than you were offered. At this point, you need to decide where the money will come from to cover college costs. The key at this stage is to find the most tax-advantaged way to pay for college costs. Student loans do have certain tax benefits, but there are limits to those benefits. It is important to understand those limits and the other options that are available. There may be other ways to pay that would have a better tax advantage. For instance, in some cases it's better for a family to increase the mortgage on their home instead of taking a student loan.

So, as you can see, a family should go through a careful planning process before calling a loan company. Before a family decides to even get a loan, the family should have done pre-planning, allocated assets according to the family's goals, filled in the financial aid applications appropriately, and developed a how-to-pay plan. If your family finds that the most tax-advantaged way to pay for college is with a student loan or a home-equity loan for a certain amount, only then is it time to call a loan company to hear what they have to offer.

Friends, Family, Neighbors

Anyone who has a kid who's gone to college is going to have an opinion about where your student should go to college and how you should pay for it. It's fine to talk to people about their experiences, but in the end you need to make up your own mind. You need to make your own college choices and your own financial decisions!

Friends and family are often ready to provide the most well-intentioned help in the world, but you need to be ready to decide if it's the right advice for you. No family has the same goals or same financial situation as your family. And it's important to consider your family's particular situation in choosing colleges and making financial decisions.

Do you remember the student named Robert who I mentioned earlier? He's the person who was orphaned and had an annuity in his name. The college of his choice had withdrawn its financial aid offer after finding out about the annuity. You may have wondered how the college learned about the annuity in the first place. This is how is happened: a well-intentioned friend of the family volunteered to help him complete his financial aid forms. The friend had some experience filling out financial aid forms and Robert readily agreed to accept his help. It was this friend who made the college aware of the annuity by including it on financial aid forms, when it should not have been included. Luckily for Robert, I was able to help him correct the situation and get the original financial aid offer reinstated. However, this provides a good lesson: it's important to get help from a qualified consultant. Family and friends may want to see you succeed with all their hearts. They may have even helped others get into college. But without a thorough understanding of your situation and how it relates to the financial aid process, their assistance can be ineffective, or, as in the case of Robert, it can even be harmful. The college choices and financial decisions they made may have worked well for their situation, but they may not work in your situation.

Sometimes it's very tempting to follow the advice of neighbors. After all, they live on the same street, so they often live in houses that have about the same value. It might seem safe to assume that neighbors would be in about the same financial situation. Imagine two families living side by side on the same street—the Owen family and the Kent family. And let's say that both families earn about the same income. The Owens just sent their son to college and the Kents have a daughter who's going to college in a year. Mr. Owens applied for financial aid for their son to go to a state college, but the family didn't receive any financial aid. Mr. Owens and Mr. Kent are out in the back yard talking about Mr. Owens' experience of getting his son into college. Mr. Kent asks, "Did you get any financial aid?"

Mr. Owens replies, "Not at all. I wish I hadn't even bothered! I filled in so much paperwork, and it was all for nothing. We didn't even get a penny. Don't waste your time!"

Let me say a few things here. First, no two families have the same financial situation. How much savings do the Kents have set aside for college? How much is their house worth and how much do they owe on their mortgage? These are just three of many important factors that have a bearing on whether or not a family gets financial aid. Second, is the college that the Owens picked the right one for the Kents? Probably not. The Owens need to consider what their daughter expects from her own college experience and consider colleges that will meet her aspirations.

Mr. Owens is still a nice guy. And it's a good idea to ask questions about his experiences. But the Owens have their own financial situation and their own goals. You need to take control of your own situation.

College Financial Aid Consultant

Of course, since I am a college financial aid consultant, I want to convince you that this is the type of person who can best guide you through the process. Still, I hope that you can see why I've decided to do this work: no other person in the admissions and financial aid process is in a position to help your family find the right college for your student at an affordable cost. During the admissions and financial aid process, your family will undoubtedly work with a number of people. Your student will work with a guidance counselor who will provide valuable assistance such as registering your student for the right high school classes, providing information about college entrance exams, and writing letters of recommendation. You will work with college financial aid officers to understand which forms their colleges require. You may decide to work with a loan officer to get a student loan. However, none of these people understands your family's goals, including the number of children you plan to send to college, your retirement plans, or how much your parents depend on you for their comfort in retirement.

> *The job of a college financial aid consultant is to consider all of your family's goals and help you afford them.*

As a college financial aid consultant, it is my job to consider all your family's goals and help you afford them. Your student's college degree should be one stepping stone in a series of financial goals. My purpose is to help you make college affordable so your student can graduate and so that your family can continue to reach the additional goals that lie ahead.

Many families regard college costs as a source of financial hardship. Without proper planning, college costs can cause hardship. However, with the right planning, your family should be much closer to all of its financial goals by the end of college. What does it take to do the right planning? It all comes down to these five steps:

1) Choose colleges that fit your needs and budget.

2) Do a pre-planning analysis of your family's

goals and financial situation and allocate your assets to maximize financial aid.

3) **Fill in all financial aid forms consistently and correctly.**

4) **Negotiate for a better financial aid package when it's appropriate.**
5) **Make a personal how-to-pay plan that covers college costs in the most tax-favored way.**

These five steps all relate to the five questions mentioned earlier in this chapter. If you think that you can guide your family through the admissions and financial aid process, then be honest with yourself...can you answer all of the questions on page 4?

You may have hoped that by the end of this book, you would be well equipped to lead your family though these five steps. I cannot guarantee that you will be able to act as your family's consultant. I cannot tell you everything you need to know in a book of this size. For instance, I can't tell you all the things you need to consider in the pre-planning analysis or what should and should not go on each line of the FAFSA. It would take much more space and be an entirely different book.

Still, by the end of this book, you should be an educated consumer. You should understand the five basic steps that your family should go through to provide your student with an affordable college education. You've already taken one giant leap toward that goal by understanding the roles and limits of the various people in the process.

I encourage you to read the rest of this book to understand what your family should do during each of the five steps. I encourage you then to find a qualified college financial aid consultant to guide your family through the details of the process. A qualified college financial aid consultant will be able to do the many things I can't hope to do in this book. What I do, and what I would expect a competent consultant to do, would be to collect all of the critical information about your family's financial situation and goals. I would provide you with recommendations for colleges that have strong programs for your student and that also tend to give good financial aid. Based on your financial information, I would fill in the financial aid forms correctly and consistently. If it's appropriate, I would help you negotiate for a better financial aid package at your student's college of choice. In the end, I would show you different ways to pay for college and help you determine the best option based on your goals and your financial situation.

Are you ready to learn how to send your student to college in an affordable way? Read on and I'll share what I've learned from years of helping families reach their goals!

POINTS TO REMEMBER

Chapter 1

Who Should You Go to for Advice?

It is important to understand the role of each player in the college financial aid process.

	Accountant	Financial Planner	FAFSA Administrator	College Financial Aid Officer	High School Guidance Counselor	Loan Company	College Financial Aid Consultant
Helps the family determine the best tax credits and deductions for college payments.	X						X
Helps the family set up appropriate investments for college once you have established your investment goals.		X					X
Provides rules and regulations for current assets.			X				X
Helps the family understand the college's financial aid application policies and procedures, and informs you of scholarship opportunities.				X			X
Helps the family consider colleges that have strong programs in your student's field of interest.					X		X
Provides loan products once the family has done careful financial aid planning.						X	X

Other than a college financial aid consultant, the people listed on the chart should not be expected to:

1) Help your family choose colleges that fit your needs and budget.

2) Reallocate funds to reduce the Expected Family Contribution.

An experienced college financial aid consultant can help you to:

1) Choose colleges that fit your needs and budget.

2) Do a pre-planning analysis of your family's goals and financial situation and allocate your assets to maximize financial aid.

3) Fill in all financial aid forms consistently and correctly.

4) Negotiate for a better financial aid package when it's appropriate.

5) Make a personal how-to-pay plan that covers college costs in the most tax-favored way.

Steps to Take Control

Find an experienced college financial aid consultant. An experienced financial aid consultant should be able to answer the following questions in a satisfactory way. Examples of satisfactory answers are provided.

1) *How can you help me choose colleges that fit my needs and budget?*

Answer: I would find out what your student is interested in studying and review your assets. We would look for colleges that have strong programs in your student's field of interest. At the same time, we would look for colleges that tend to give students like yours good financial aid. [Read Chapter 2 for a more thorough description of the process that I follow.]

2) *What is the most common way of reducing the Expected Family Contribution?*

Answer: The most common way is to reposition student or parent assets to places that do not count against a family in the Expected Family Contribution (EFC) calculation. *[For your information: It is not always beneficial for a family to move assets. If done incorrectly, this can have legal and tax consequences. Don't just move money. Understand the process first. Read Chapter 3 for more information about the financial planning process.]*

3) *How would you help me submit my financial aid forms correctly and on time?*

Answer: We would make financial estimates and enter them consistently on all financial aid applications. As soon as you are finished with your federal tax forms, we would submit revisions to the applications. *[Chapter 4 provides a more detailed description of this process.]*

4) *When is it appropriate to negotiate for a better financial aid package? How would you do it?*

Answer: It's appropriate to negotiate for better financial aid when the college of your choice has made an offer that is low for a student like yours. The best way to negotiate is to provide documented information to make the college aware of the shortfall in their package. *[Chapter 5 contains further advice regarding negotiations.]*

5) *What would you do to help me determine the best way to pay for college?*

<u>Answer:</u> I would review your assets and consider your financial goals. We would look for a way that would provide the best financial aid and the maximum tax advantage. *[More details are provided in Chapter 6.]*

Chapter 2

Choose Colleges That Fit Your Needs And Budget

This chapter focuses on the admissions counseling that I do with students. Some people might wonder why I deal with admissions counseling in a book about college financial aid. I have found admissions counseling to be a valuable part of my work with families. When I first started my business, I focused only on guiding families through the college financial aid process and relied on my clients to make college choices with the help of their school guidance counselor. I found that about 30% of the students wanted to transfer out of the colleges they had selected. I was faced with a problem: I was succeeding at helping families get financial aid, but students were dissatisfied with their college experience. What I realized was that I needed to help students define what they wanted from college and help them select colleges that would satisfy their expectations. After I started helping families with the admissions process as well, student satisfaction increased enormously. In the last few years, generally 99 out of 100 students who I worked with were satisfied with the college they selected. This chapter describes the process that I rely on to help families choose a college that meets their needs.

Understand What the Student Expects from College

To start the process of choosing a college, the student needs to be clear about what he or she expects from the college experience. Once I've met a family, I like to ask to have some time alone with the student so that I can learn his or her expectations of college. This is what I ask the student to do: ***Imagine the perfect college experience for you and tell me about it.***

Those students who are prepared to go to college are able to tell me what they've been thinking about without much further prompting. If a student wants to enter a certain profession, then they let me know they want to be a doctor or a lawyer or a teacher. They usually go on to tell me the types of experiences they want to have to prepare for that profession. Students who are interested in sports will tell me they want to go to a college with a strong football team or basketball team. The student might be looking for an avenue to the professional leagues or just for some fun and excitement during their college years. Or the student might just want to go to a college where he or she can be a spectator at a big game each weekend.

During my discussions with students, I can usually tell whether or not they are ready to go to college. Those who are ready will be able to give me some clear expectations, even if they are not sure what they want to study. For instance, one young woman recently told me that her perfect college would be a small school where she'd get to know her professors well and see them when she needed help. She's been playing soccer in high school and she considers that a big part of her life, so she wants to continue playing soccer in college. She isn't sure what she wants to study, but she has clearly been thinking about going to college and has some expectations in mind. She is ready to go to college.

On the other hand, I recently spoke to a young man who could not tell me what the perfect college would look like. He couldn't tell me what activities he'd like to do at college or what he wanted to study. When I asked him why he wanted to go to college, he said, "Because my parents want me to." This young man was not ready to benefit from a college experience. To benefit from college, a student should WANT to go to college. I had to advise his parents that their son didn't seem ready to attend college. I suggested that it might be better for him to take some time after high school graduation to find a job, do some volunteer work, get into a trade like plumbing, enter a program at a technical school, or consider the military.

At the other extreme of the spectrum, I sometimes talk to students who are too focused on going to one specific college. For instance, when I asked one young man to imagine his perfect college, he told me, "Duke—that's my perfect college. That's the one for me!" By discussing what he liked about Duke, I was able to find out what he liked about the big name university experience. I helped him identify several other universities that would give him the same type of experience. He applied to four universities in addition to Duke. In the end, he didn't get accepted at Duke, but all four of the other universities accepted him and provided excellent financial aid offers.

Let me tell you about another student who was too focused on one type of school. One mother came in with her daughter who was determined to attend an Ivy League college. The daughter's grades were quite good—she was on the honor roll every term, but she was not taking many difficult classes. She was also in some clubs, but she did not demonstrate the kind of leadership that the Ivy League schools typically look for. Basically, she was a good student, but she did not fit the Ivy League profile. After the young woman told me her plans to apply to four Ivy League schools, I asked her what she would do if she were not accepted to any of them. She said that was not going to happen. I asked her to just imagine if it were to happen, what would she do? She refused to even think of it. All I could do was advise her to apply to some additional colleges, just in case she was not accepted at her dream schools. She was back in my office four months later with tears in her eyes because she did not take my advice and she had not been accepted to any of the four Ivy League schools. We talked further about what she expected from her college experience. Based on her description, I selected two colleges for her. I also gave her a list of schools that met her expectations and advised her to select two additional schools from the list. She applied to four schools that I recommended and was accepted to all four of them. She was offered a full tuition scholarship by one college which is where she decided to go. Once the daughter had dropped her expectation of going to a highly prestigious school, it was gratifying to work with her. We were able to discuss and define what she wanted from her college experience. Then we were able to focus on schools where she was a strong applicant and get her a generous amount of financial aid.

Many parents think that they are good at understanding what their student wants out of college. However, there is one serious weakness that parents can have: parents sometimes impose their wishes on their children. One example of this was Ms. Cooper who brought her daughter Brenda to me after Brenda had failed out of college in the first term. Brenda was a bright person, who shouldn't have failed out. Ms. Cooper brought Brenda so that I could give her guidance. Brenda had been a business major, so when I learned that she had taken a course called Introduction to Business, I expected that would have been the easiest class for her. Instead, Brenda told me, "That was the hardest class I've ever taken." When I spoke to Brenda alone, I learned that Brenda had become a business major to please her mother. She actually enjoyed drawing. Ms. Cooper had never told Brenda to become a business major, but she had made it clear that Brenda should do something that would earn a good salary. She had told Brenda, "You need to make money. You need to support yourself and you're not going to do it with those drawings." As it turned out, both Ms. Cooper and her daughter needed guidance!

After Ms. Cooper came back into my office, I asked her if she realized that Brenda had felt pressured into choosing business as a major, and that Brenda had failed her courses because she was not interested in them. Ms. Cooper broke down into tears and apologized to Brenda, who in turn cried and apologized for not telling her mother before. After that, Brenda entered community college, where she took some art courses. Her drawings were astounding! She clearly had a passion for drawing, which she developed into a career in fashion design. As with most people, Brenda performed well in college when she studied what she enjoyed. And furthermore, she was able to cultivate her talent and use it to launch a lucrative career. Although parents might not be able to make a connection between their student's interests and a secure career, it's usually easier for students to reach that goal if they pursue their interests.

When students tell me about their perfect college experience, I like to listen to their full description before asking for any details. This helps me to understand what is most important to each student. Still, by the end of each discussion, I need to understand two important things: the environment where a student wants to study and the programs the student wants to participate in. Some students may focus more on the setting; others may focus more on what they want to study. If a student hasn't told me about either the environment or the programs they want, then I need to inquire about them. Here are two lists of the basic things I need to know before I can help students pick colleges.

ENVIRONMENT	PROGRAMS
In what region of the country does the student want to live?	What does the student want to study?
In what type of location does the student want to live —country, suburb, or city?	What types of internships does the student want?
	What sport does the student want to play or watch?
Should classes all be within walking distance or is it okay to take a bus?	What club activities does the student want to participate in?

Continued on next page

ENVIRONMENT (CON'T)	PROGRAMS (CON'T)
What size should the college be— small, medium, or large? And what does small, medium or large mean to that student? What style of campus does the student prefer — traditional or contemporary?	What church or faith-based organizations does the student want to participate in? What type of diversity does the student want? What type of arts or drama programs does the student enjoy? Does the student want to study abroad? Where?

The questions are in no particular order. The importance of each factor depends on the student. Some students might find it important to go to a school in the city with easy access to art exhibits or drama performances. Others might want to go to a college with a strong religious affiliation that has faith-based clubs and activities. It all depends on the student's expectations.

The key to starting the college search right is to understand what your student expects the experience to be like. It's important for parents to listen to their son or daughter and avoid imposing expectations on them. Of course, you should expect your student to study with dedication and get good grades. You should expect them to gain the types of experiences that will help them succeed after they graduate. Still, students should be able to pursue studies that interest them. Otherwise, they'll probably find it hard to devote the time and energy needed, just as Brenda did when she failed out of her business courses. That's why I ask students to imagine the perfect college. It gives them a chance to describe the aspects of the college experience that they value the most. Once I understand what the student wants, I can begin suggesting colleges that will offer that type of experience.

Select Colleges

Once I have a clear idea of what a student wants from college, I help families select colleges based on three important factors:

1) Environment of the college
2) Programs offered by the college
3) Financial match between the family and the college

The first two factors come from the student's expectations. The financial match between the college and the family is more complicated. Part of it depends on the pre-planning analysis, which I discuss in detail in Chapter 3. The pre-planning analysis determines how much a family in your financial situation would be expected to pay for college. The other part of the financial match depends on the college's costs and its tendency to provide financial aid to families and students like yours. Basically, a good financial match occurs when a college requires you to pay less than you are able to pay.

It's relatively easy to find out if a college has the right programs and environment. There are several college guides that describe all the important aspects of colleges. Search engines are an even better tool for finding colleges that meet your needs. I prefer search engines to printed guides because the search engines are more efficient. Whether you use a search engine or a printed guide, it's critical to use one that is as comprehensive as possible. Avoid college guides that focus on the "best colleges" or the "top colleges." These guides tend to focus on several hundred colleges that have good reputations. Good reputations often go along with less financial aid. According to Digest of Education Statistics, there were 4,216 degree-granting institutions in the

United States during the 2004–05 school year. That means that a college guide with information on 500 colleges leaves out about 3,700. There's a good chance that the guide will leave out colleges that will meet your student's expectations and provide a good financial match, especially since the guides tend to include colleges and universities with higher costs and less opportunity for aid.

It's more difficult to find a college that's a good financial match. You won't actually know until you've received a financial aid offer several weeks or even several months after you've been accepted to the college. Still, given a college's history of providing financial aid, an experienced college financial aid consultant can help you identify colleges that are likely to be a good financial match. Most of the families who come to me earn too much to receive need-based financial aid. Our goal is then to maximize merit-based financial aid, which is based on a student's academic performance.

The key to finding colleges that will probably make a good merit-based financial aid offer is to find those where your student is an attractive applicant. High grades and high college admissions scores are what usually make an applicant attractive. Search engines and college guides usually provide the score ranges of the middle 50% of a college's incoming freshmen. The score is used as a measure of the college's academic standards. Schools with high academic standards have high score ranges. Once your student has taken a college admissions test, it's easy to tell where he or she stands among the pool of applicants. When using the SAT, many colleges look at the sum of the critical reading and the math scores. I encourage parents to use their student's SAT or ACT score to classify colleges into one of three categories: financial safety, financial target, and financial reach. These classifications are summarized on the following table.

COLLEGE CLASSIFICATION	DEFINITION	CHANCES OF GETTING AID
FINANCIAL SAFETY COLLEGE	Your student's SAT/ACT test score is greater than the college's middle 50% score range, putting the student in the top 25% of applicants.	Your student has a high chance of receiving good merit-based financial aid.
FINANCIAL TARGET COLLEGE	Your student's SAT/ACT score is within the college's middle 50% score range.	Student may receive some merit-based financial aid.
FINANCIAL REACH COLLEGE	Your student's SAT/ACT score is below the college's middle 50% score range, putting the student among the bottom 25% of applicants.	Student will likely not receive merit-based financial aid.

Let's say that your student earned a combined SAT critical reading and math score of 1100. Now let's compare that to the SAT scores of the middle 50% of admitted freshmen from three colleges. If the middle 50% for one college is 900 to 1070, that would be a financial safety college. Your student has a better score than the middle 50%, so your student would be an attractive applicant and would probably receive a good merit-based financial aid offer and an excellent need-based package if applicable. If a second college has a score range of 1050 to 1150, that would be a financial target college. Your student might receive some financial aid, but it will probably not be as good as the aid offered to applicants with scores above the middle 50%. If another college has a score range of 1190 to 1300, that would be a reach college. A student with a SAT score of 1100 would probably not receive merit-based financial aid.

I advise students to apply to several financial safety colleges and several financial target colleges. It's fine to apply to one or two reach schools, but if you want to maximize merit-based financial aid, financial safety and target colleges should be the focus of your search. This may contradict the advice that you heard in the past. In fact, when I was applying to college, my high school counselor told me to apply to two reach colleges, two target colleges, and two safety colleges. However, my high school counselor defined target, reach, and safety schools much differently: she was thinking in terms of admissions instead of financial aid. To her, a reach college was a place that I would love to attend but probably would not accept me. A target college was a place I'd love to attend and would probably accept me. A safety school was a place that would definitely accept me but that I really did not want to attend. The idea was that I would only go to the safety school if I wasn't accepted at a reach or a target school. These days, that's a fine way to do things . . . as long as you're wealthy. For the vast majority of middle-class Americans, the cost of college is a significant expense. It makes sense to put your effort into finding financial safety and target schools that meet your student's expectations. These are the colleges that will most likely make good merit-based financial aid offers. They are also more likely to provide excellent need-based award packages if your family qualifies.

> *Most families should focus on selecting financial safety and target colleges. These will offer the best financial aid.*

I cannot over-emphasize the importance of selecting financial safety and target schools. I recently worked with the Turner family, who had chosen schools before coming to me.

Mrs. Turner had done a good job of understanding her son John's expectations and she'd spent hours going through college guides to find colleges that suited his interests. She had selected about ten colleges, all of which happened to be on U.S. News list of top colleges. None of the colleges she'd selected were in the Ivy League, but all of them had high academic standards. Given John's grades and SAT scores, he might have been admitted to some of the colleges, but I am confident that he would not have received any merit-based financial aid. The Turners would not have had enough income or savings to afford the cost of these colleges. I advised them to apply to some financial target schools, where they might get some merit-based aid. More importantly, I helped them select three or four financial safety colleges, where the family will definitely get $10,000 or $15,000, even $20,000 of merit-based aid.

If your family is wealthy, then it's fine to focus on reach schools. For the majority of middle-class Americans, it's wiser to focus on financial safety and target colleges. These are the colleges that want to attract your student. These are the colleges that will offer your family better financial aid.

Help Your Student Be an Attractive Applicant

The student needs to be as attractive as possible to the college. First of all, students need to prepare themselves throughout high school to be competitive college applicants. Good grades, participation in extra-curricular activities, and high college admissions scores are all valuable.

Both good grades and college entrance scores are important for admissions and financial aid. A student with high test scores and low grades will be perceived as unmotivated. Although an admissions office may regard grades more heavily when making admissions decisions, financial aid is often based more heavily on standardized test scores. First of all, the standardized tests are regarded as a fair way of comparing students who have passed through a variety of school systems. Secondly, it's much easier to rank students and allocate available money by using standardized test scores. If your student has trouble performing well on the SAT or ACT college admissions tests, it may be well worth the investment to pay for a test preparation class or tutor. The resulting increase in test scores could lead to thousands of additional dollars in financial aid.

Throughout high school, it is also important to pursue extra-curricular activities. A student should have an interest and find ways of pursuing it. If a student has been taking Spanish for five years and is planning to major in Spanish, then the student should be doing something else to develop his interest. Maybe there's an active Spanish Club in school. If so, then the student should try to assume a leadership role in the club and ensure that the club runs meaningful activities. For instance, the club could sponsor a Cinco de Mayo celebration in the school to raise interest in Spanish culture. If there is a large Spanish-speaking community in the area, then the club might provide translation services to members of the community or provide tutoring services to local children in Spanish. Students need to do some type of extra-curricular activity that shows they are truly interested in the subject and that helps them develop the interest further. Classroom activities alone are not enough.

In addition to developing an area of interest, I also recommend that students explore. They should try doing something out of the ordinary, even if they think they will only do it for a short time. For instance, they could try taking a class at an evening school in painting, photography, or creative writing. If there's a summer school program, they might try something like archery or karate. If they haven't done volunteer work before, then they might try doing some work at Habitat for Humanity or in a local soup kitchen. If they don't like it, they don't have to do it again. However, what sometimes happens is that they find that helping other people is fun and they decide to continue. Trying new activities and doing volunteer work helps a person keep a sense of discovery alive and shows a willingness to learn new ideas.

College Visits: Which colleges are a good fit?

The college visit is a two-way street: the student is there to learn about the college and the college wants to learn about the student. The student should use college visits to see how well each college measures up against his or her idea of the perfect college. At the same time, the student should use the visit to promote himself or herself as a desirable applicant.

The student should always make appointments ahead of time. I recommend taking a campus tour first and then having a consultation with an admissions counselor. Campus tours are often given by college students who are juniors or seniors. If you know what you want to study, it's a good idea to ask for a tour guide who majors in that area. Before visiting the college, review your description of a perfect college, then look at the college's web site and remind yourself why you chose to visit this college. During the campus tour, ask about the features of the college that are most important for you. You need to decide whether the college meets your expectations.

When you meet with the admissions counselor, think of it as an information session rather than an interview. The admissions counselor wants to find students who will benefit from the college. If you have unanswered questions from the tour, this is a good time to get answers. Your questions will help the counselor understand what you want from college. Knowing your expectations will be a real advantage because you will be able to share the features of the college that attract you to the campus and that would make it an enjoyable place to study. If you were attracted by a specific program, such as a special teacher training program or a program for women scientists, be certain to let the admissions counselor know. Be prepared to discuss your interests and how the college will help you pursue those interests. College counselors are as interested in finding applicants who will thrive in their college as you are in finding a college that will meet your needs.

It's a good idea to make a personal connection with an admissions officer at each college where you plan to apply. Make sure that you get the admissions counselor's business card with a postal address, an email address, and a phone number. Many admissions officers follow up an interview with a form letter or a small note. Very few students reply. If you like the college and you plan to apply, then take the time to write a reply. Any written correspondence will be included in your admissions file. A handwritten letter to the admissions officer would show a genuine interest in the college and would certainly be noticed. In fact, there is some indication that college admissions offices are keeping track of student contacts for use in final decisions.

At some later time, you may have some follow-up questions about the admissions process or about some aspect of a certain program. The admissions counselor will be a valuable resource. As long as you have sincere and meaningful questions, the counselor will regard them favorably as a sign of your eagerness to attend the college. It's important not to pester the counselor with unnecessary questions and to use the right method of communication for whatever question you have. For instance, if you have a question that could be answered quickly, then a phone call would be appropriate. If it's a question that might require the counselor to talk with someone else, then an email would make more sense.

As a college financial aid consultant, I like to make sure

that students use college visits to test their description of a perfect college. If a student has told me that she wants to go to a college in the country and she doesn't like two colleges she visited because she says they're "out in the middle of nowhere," then we need to revise her description of the perfect college. Specifically, I would want to know what she would be missing by living in those country settings. Based on that information, we would review her list of potential colleges and continue the college search. By the time that she starts filling in applications, she needs to identify several safety and target schools that meet her expectations.

Highlight Student Strengths in the Application

Students often find it hard to write about themselves in an interesting way. I encourage students to write about their activities in relationship to their central interest, whatever that interest may be. That interest should be the central theme of the essay and everything else should contribute to that theme. By the time a student starts selecting colleges, we have usually identified an area of interest. After all, that's what leads to the college selections.

When a student has a hard time getting started on an essay, I set aside time to discuss his or her interests. Together, we develop the central theme and the supporting ideas. One student of mine wasn't sure what he wanted to study when we first met. During my initial meeting with him, I asked him what he does that he would call a passion. He said that he loves to write music and lyrics. I asked him what instrument he played and he told me he could play everything. As it turned out, he was quite serious about playing everything. He had created a CD with six different tracks in which he played keyboard, guitar, drums and other instruments. He was his own band! He eventually decided to make music the focus of his studies. When he wrote his application essay, he linked every activity that he wrote about to the central theme of his interest in music. He wrote one paragraph about the CDs he had made, one about how he enjoyed teaching people to play instruments, and another about the relationship between his love of music and his enjoyment of math and science. In the end, he described how the college of his choice would help him pursue his interest in music.

How will the particular college you are applying to help you pursue your interest? That should be one aspect of the essay. The information you gained from college visits should feed right into your essay. During each college visit, you've been observing the features of each college that meet your expectations. In the application, it's important to highlight those features and explain how they will help you reach your goals.

Admissions counselors do like creativity, but it's important not to write anything risky in the application. For instance, one student I worked with was an excellent writer who had participated in her school's literary magazine for several years. In fact, she became one of the magazine's editors during her senior year. This experience along with good grades made her a good candidate for one college that had a well-known literary magazine. The application essay asked students to write about the value of being brief. Instead of writing a regular essay, she took a big risk by writing only a quote from Shakespeare: Brevity is the soul of wit (from Hamlet, Act 2, Scene 2). When she consulted me about this, I told her that it would be much better to use the quote as part of a full-length essay. I tried to persuade her that she should not rely on the fact that she had numerous stories accepted in her high school's literary magazine. A full-length essay would demonstrate her talent at writing and make her a desirable candidate. Despite my advice, she submitted the brief quote. As it turned out, she was not accepted at that college.

Although we do not know exactly why, it may very well be that the essay did not do the desired job.

If you're not sure whether you have a good idea for an essay, ask yourself:

- Does this idea demonstrate bad judgment?

- Could this possibly offend someone?

If the answer to either of these questions is yes, then write about something else.

In the end, the college application is one more step along the selection process. During the first stage of the selection process, students need to define what they want from college. After that, the college financial aid consultant suggests affordable colleges that provide the expected types of environment and programs. Students then visit colleges to see which ones provide the best fit with their expectations. In the end, students should be able to describe how the college of their choice will help them meet their goals. The application essay should show how well the college fits the needs of the student.

POINTS TO REMEMBER

Chapter 2

Choose Colleges That Fit Your Needs And Budget

- A student should want to go to college. If your student does not want to go to college, it might be better for the student to try something else after high school, such as getting a job, entering a trade, entering a program at a technical school, or joining the military.

- The family should select colleges based on three important factors: college environment, college programs, and financial match between the family and the college.

- Students should focus on selecting schools with programs and an environment that will satisfy their expectations instead of focusing on attending one specific college. This will increase the chances of getting a good financial aid package.

- A good financial match occurs when a college requires you to pay less than you are able to pay. An experienced college financial aid consultant can help you identify colleges that are likely to be a good financial match.

- The key to finding colleges that will probably make a good merit-based financial aid offer is to find those where your student is an attractive applicant. High grades and admissions scores plus participation in extra-curricular activities make an applicant attractive.

- If your family is wealthy, then it may be fine to focus on reach schools. For the majority of middle-class Americans, it's wiser to focus on financial safety and target colleges. These are the colleges that want to attract your student and will offer your family better financial aid.

Steps to Take Control

- The key to starting the college search right is to understand what the student expects the experience to be like. The parents and student should take time to discuss what the student expects to learn and do at college.

- The parents should work with the student to select several financial safety colleges and several financial target colleges. This will increase the chances of getting good financial aid.

- How good are the student's grades? If they are lower than expected, then extra help from teachers or tutoring may be helpful.

- The student should be familiar with the questions on college admissions tests and strategies for answering them correctly. Use a study guide or enter a preparation program.

- What extra-curricular activities does the student participate in? Does the student have any leadership roles, such as club treasurer or team captain? The student should pick one or two interests and get involved.

- Visit colleges. The student should use college visits to see how well each college measures up against his or her idea of the perfect college. At the same time, the student should use the visit to promote himself or herself as a desirable applicant.

- The student should make a personal connection with an admissions officer at each college. When you have follow-up questions about the admissions process or about some aspect of a certain program, contact the same admissions officer.

- In the end, students should be able to describe how the college of their choice will help them meet their goals. The application essay should show how well the college fits the needs of the student.

Chapter 3

Pre-Planning Analysis

The two features of my service that help families the most are the guidance in picking affordable colleges and guidance in planning how to pay for college. Now that we've discussed how to pick colleges, let's start talking about paying for college.

Most of my clients are middle-class families who believe that they earn too much to qualify for financial aid. They are often surprised by the amount of money they save by reallocating funds and maximizing financial aid. The combination of pre-planning and choosing the correct college can have dramatic financial benefits.

Many families come to me looking for means other than financial aid to finance college. They often have pre-conceived ideas of how they are going to pay. Some are planning to use their home equity; others are planning to rely on student loans. Depending on the family's situation, these might not be the best options. My job is to help families consider all of their options and help them see the impact of each option on their financial goals.

So, what do you need to do to maximize your financial aid? The answer depends on your family's financial situation. I help each family arrive at a plan through what I call the Pre-Planning Analysis. During this analysis, I collect the financial information that the family will be submitting to colleges. Then I calculate the amount of money that colleges would expect the family to pay each year if the family did not do any further planning. That's why I call this the Pre-Planning Analysis. Before doing any financial aid planning, I determine how much money colleges would expect the family to pay. Once we have completed the Pre-Planning Analysis, I provide the family with options that they can follow to maximize their eligibility for financial aid. I always present these as financial options because, in the end, the family needs to decide if the options will help them reach their financial goals.

Pre-planning is designed to answer these questions:

1) *What is the family's current financial situation?*

2) *What are the family's financial goals?*

3) *To what extent does a family currently qualify for college financial aid?*

4) *What can the family do to maximize eligibility for financial aid?*

By the end of the pre-planning process, the family should have a clear plan for allocating money for college and other major goals, such as retirement.

Understand the Goal:
Reduce Your Expected Family Contribution

When I take a family through the pre-planning analysis, I look at the family's assets as if I were a college financial aid officer. I am looking to see how much money colleges would expect the family to pay.

Colleges collect information about the family's assets through financial aid forms. Most colleges require the FAFSA (Free Application for Federal Student Aid). Other colleges use the FAFSA and CSS/Financial Aid PROFILE. And in addition, some colleges have their own financial aid forms. No matter what form or forms a college uses to collect information, the basic equation is the same:

The cost of attendance is calculated by adding the costs of tuition, room, board, fees, books, and living expenses. The Expected Family Contribution is a key term that I will use throughout the rest of this chapter. **The Expected Family Contribution is the minimum amount that a college would expect you to pay each year**. Colleges determine this amount by collecting information about the family's assets via the FAFSA and/or other forms and applying a formula to see how much money the family should be expected to pay. Once a college has calculated the Expected Family Contribution, the college subtracts that amount from the Cost of Attendance to determine the family's Financial Need. That is the amount that the school will attempt to provide through grants, loans, and student work study.

As a college financial aid consultant, one of my main goals is to help your family reduce your Expected Family Contribution. This is one purpose of the pre-planning analysis.

Assess Your Current Financial Situation

The first step of the pre-planning analysis is to assess a family's current financial situation. I have two objectives when I do this. One is to find out about all of the assets that could be used to pay for college. The second is to find out how the family is actually planning to use each of the assets.

To get information about the family's assets, I ask the parent's to provide me with all the financial statements that would be used to fill in the college financial aid applications. It is important to review the assets of the parents and the student because that is what is required on the college financial aid forms. The following table provides a list of the financial statements that I review.

INCOME STATEMENTS	■ Latest federal tax return ■ W-2 forms
INVESTMENT STATEMENTS	■ Retirement investments (401k, 403B, pensions, annuities) ■ Non-retirement investments (checking accounts, savings accounts, CDs, stocks, bonds, whole life insurance, etc.)
HOME & AUTO STATEMENTS	■ Mortgage information for any houses ■ Homeowner's policy declaration page for each house ■ Auto policy declaration page

When working with a family, I ask them to bring in all of their statements. As we go through them, I ask how the family is planning to use each of the assets. For instance, if a family has a second house, I'll ask why they have a second house. If the parents want to move to that house when they retire, then I know it's probably not an option to sell the second house to finance college. On the other hand, if the house was purchased as an investment property, then it's more likely that the family would consider selling it to pay for college.

OK, maybe your family doesn't have a second house. (Most of us don't!) Still, if you have money set aside in a savings account or a CD, or if you have other assets, it's important for me to know what you plan to do with them. That way, I can understand whether each asset could possibly be used to pay for college.

Consider Your Family's Goals

Once I have an overview of the family's assets, I ask about the family's financial goals. It's important to consider all of the family's major goals, such as the number of children who may go to college, the age at which the parents plan to retire, and care that may need to be provided for aging grandparents.

Another aim of this discussion is to help parents understand that their financial decisions affect their ability to finance college. So, for example, if parents tell me that they don't have enough money to pay for college, yet they just went out and got a $600 per month lease on a Lexus, they need to understand that the lease on the Lexus could prevent them from paying for college. Likewise, the family should understand that the financial decisions they make about college affect their ability to finance other goals. For instance, a family might have to sacrifice substantial retirement savings to send their student to a college that costs $50,000 a year out-of-pocket. However, the family might be able to set aside enough money for retirement if they send their student to a college that costs only $30,000 a year out-of-pocket.

One important function of this discussion is to help the parents and the student understand their expectations about paying for college and then see if those expectations are practical. Some parents want to pay everything for college; other parents don't want to pay a dime. Most parents are somewhere in the middle: they want to share the cost of college with their students. Even if the parents can pay for 100% of the student's education, I find it's better to have the student shoulder some of the costs. First, it helps the student take studies more seriously. Second, paying off loans helps the student gain a good credit score. As a college financial aid consultant, I need to know how much college expense the parents are willing to take on, and then I can help the family adjust those expectations, if necessary.

Let's take one extreme example in which the parents were being over-protective of their daughter. Mr. and Mrs. Benning had a daughter named Rose, who was an only child, and everything that the parents did was designed to set Rose up for success. They had a substantial amount of savings for her college education and for their retirement. The parent's plan was to move and retire in the area where Rose would go to college. Once Rose graduated from college, they wanted to set her up in business. Financially, Mr. and Mrs. Benning could have followed this plan, but I advised them not to. The college years are the time when Rose is preparing to step out into the world on her own. If Mr. and Mrs. Benning do everything for her, then she's not going to be well prepared when she has to face a situation on her own. After discussing this, Mr. and Mrs. Benning decided to revise their plan. In the end, they let Rose move off to college without following her. Regarding finances, the family needed to take out $20,000 in student loans to cover the cost of the four years of education. The parents decided to pay the interest on the loans while Rose is at college, but have Rose pay the principal after she graduated. Not only will this help the parents in their retirement, it will help Rose gain the skills she needs to become independent.

> *Financial planning should involve all of the family's major goals, including:*
> *1) Number of children going to college*
> *2) Retirement plans*
> *3) Care for grandparents*

Some parents want to pay for 100% of their student's costs, but doing so might risk their ability to pay their mortgage or save for retirement. In this case, I advise the family that the student is benefitting from this education and it would be reasonable for the student to pay for some of it, whether it be through student loans or a part-time job. The Clark family was in this situation. The Clarks had a son named Ted who wanted to be an actor. The parents were concerned that it would be difficult for Ted to earn a living as an actor, so they reached a compromise: Ted would be a business major, but he would go to college in Los Angeles, California, where he could easily audition for acting positions on the side. Mr. and Mrs. Clark came to me after Ted had entered his first year of college. The high school guidance counselor had advised the Clarks to take out a Parent Plus loan to cover the $38,000 in uncovered expenses for the first year of college. If the parents had continued following this plan, they would have accumulated over $150,000 worth of loans by the time Ted graduated. This would have prevented Mr. and Mrs. Clark from saving for retirement, and it might have even made it difficult for them to keep up with their mortgage payments. On top of that, what motivation did Ted have to study hard and earn his business degree in four years? What would compel him to find a job in the area of business if acting didn't work out for him? After discussing the situation, the Clarks decided that it would be wise to use student loans to cover as much of the remaining college costs as possible. This would help Ted see that he needed to develop a career with good income, and it would help the parents continue to meet their living expenses and save for retirement.

I cannot overemphasize the importance of having students take some of the financial responsibility for their education. Not only is it good for parents; it is good for students. How many students have reported that things are going fine at college, when they are actually missing classes and assignments? How many unsuspecting parents have thought that their child was performing well at college, only to receive an academic probation notice in the mail? Or, even worse, I know of a mother who learned that her daughter had failed all of her classes during the first semester only after driving her daughter for nine hours to college for the second semester!

Of course, I wish the best for the Clark family, and I hope that Ted focuses on his studies. I admire the family for reaching a practical compromise that allows Ted to follow his dream of becoming an actor, yet give him the skills to follow a career in business if acting does not work out. Ted may have been sincere when he promised to study business. Still, if Ted isn't paying for any of his education, what reason does he have to take his business courses seriously? Those classes aren't costing him anything! From his perspective, it's to his benefit to spend as much time as possible going to auditions. Even if he has to miss a few business classes to attend auditions, so what? For him, the goal is to get his foot into acting so that he doesn't need to fall back on a job pushing papers for some company, right? I think my point is clear: letting Ted pay for some of his education will help him to value those business classes and encourage him to get his money's worth from them.

At the opposite side of the spectrum, I have met with parents who did not want to pay for any of their student's college education. If the family's income is low enough, then they might qualify for enough need-based aid to make this possible. However, it's going to be difficult for a student in a middle-class family to cover the cost of education at a 4-year college on his or her own, unless that student is gifted enough to earn a comprehensive scholarship. Full scholarships are rare these days, even for exceptionally gifted students. If parents are not willing to pay anything, the student will most likely need to attend a community college for the first two years, and then get a full-time job to earn a bachelor's degree through part-time studies. Most parents who meet me are willing to finance part of their student's education. However, in several instances, one parent wanted to pay for part of college, while the other parent did not. My first goal in that situation is to understand why the parents have differing expectations. Then, I let the parents know that they need to agree on their approach to financing their student's education; otherwise, I cannot help them. As a college financial aid consultant, I present families with their options for choosing colleges and paying their costs. The parents need to agree on the resources that they are willing to devote to college, or they will not benefit from my advice.

As a college financial aid consultant, once I know what the parent's expectations are, I can help them determine if those expectations are reasonable. If the parents are earning $100,000 per year and they want to pay the total cost of sending their student to a $50,000 a year college, I need to help them determine if that's a realistic expectation. For a family that's paying a mortgage and saving for retirement, it would probably not be realistic. On the other hand, it would be realistic for a family that has already paid off their mortgage and put away significant savings for retirement. As you can see, other financial goals have an impact on college financial goals. A family that needs to save for retirement and pay a mortgage should not devote so much money toward college that they cannot continue saving for retirement and paying for the house. Those other goals are just as important.

Consider Major Life Events

When I sit down with a family, we need to discuss their current financial situation, and we also need to consider any major life events that would increase or decrease the family's income. Some of the most common major life events are retirement, changing jobs, having another child, and the passing of grandparents.

Obviously, it's important to anticipate events that will reduce the family's income because any decrease in income can have an impact on the family's ability to achieve financial goals. For instance, I'm working with the Gibson family, in which the mother is expecting to have her fourth child at the age of 41. This will have an impact on the Gibsons' income because the mother is planning to leave her job for a period of time. Their first child is just about to enter college and the parents will have to pay for college for the first three children over the course of ten years. Pre-planning is making the family's goals easier to achieve and certainly reducing stress. When the Gibsons initially approached me, they believed that their college savings plan would pay for 100% of the education for all four of their children. Through the pre-planning analysis, I discovered that they would be able to pay for the first child's education with their savings, but the savings would not cover costs for the second and third child. As a result of pre-planning, the parents now realize that they need to take advantage of other options even when paying for the first child's education. They have several options available: student loans, parent loans, and home equity. I will help them determine the right mix of options when it comes time to pay. But what's important is this: during pre-planning the Gibsons took into account the mother's time off from work and determined that their college savings plan would not suffice. Without pre-planning, the Gibsons would have depleted their savings while their first child was at college and scrambled to finance college for the second and third child. Now the Gibsons will be able to allocate their resources wisely, take advantage of other financing options, and make college affordable for all of their children.

It may not be so obvious, but it is just as important to anticipate events that will increase the family's income. For instance, Mr. Morgan had been a police officer for twenty-four years. After one more year of service, he was planning to retire at the age of 50 and work as a security consultant. Once he retired, he would be receiving a pension in addition to earning income from his business as a consultant. Overall, his family would probably see an increase in income. Mr. and Mrs. Morgan were planning to send two children through college in a period of seven years. In this particular instance, we focused on picking the appropriate colleges so that the students qualified for as much merit-based aid as possible. We also looked at options for maximizing the parents' income. In this case, the Morgan family paid for college on a tax-favored basis, making more money available for mortgage payments and retirement. Without pre-planning, Mr. and Mrs. Morgan would have devoted too much of their income towards college costs.

Another situation when it's important to anticipate an increase is in the case where a family that receives need-based aid receives an inheritance. Several families have come to me with the same problem after receiving inheritances. The situation is this: the student has been receiving a certain amount of need-based financial aid, when a grandparent passes away. As you may know, the FAFSA has to be submitted each year to qualify for financial aid. Well, when a family enters an inheritance on the FAFSA, the inheritance is going to raise the EFC and reduce the financial aid. Let me describe two ways in which this can be handled.

The first way of handling the situation is to miss one year of financial aid, place the inheritance in a shelter, and then apply for financial aid again the following year. This is the strategy that the Slater family used. The Slater family had two children going through college in a period of six years. The first child was in college when a grandparent passed away and left an inheritance nearly all of which was stock. By the time the Slaters came to see me, they had reported the inheritance on the FAFSA and their EFC had jumped from $8,000 per year to $25,000 per year. Due to the inheritance, the family no longer qualified for $17,000 in need-based aid. If the family had continued to hold the inheritance as stock, they would have needed to use the inheritance to pay for college for the next five years. It was too late to help the Slaters recover their need-based aid that year. However, I advised the Slaters to sell the stock and shelter the funds. Since the sheltered assets do not count against a family for financial aid purposes, the family was able to receive need-based aid again during the following four years. Instead of paying $68,000 of the inheritance money to the college, they were able to hold onto it for retirement. That's the power of planning!

Under the circumstances, we resolved the Slaters' situation well. The family used only $17,000 of the inheritance to pay for one year of college costs, instead of paying $85,000 over five years. Still, it would have been even better if the parents had made a plan for the inheritance ahead of time. With the right planning, we could have sheltered the inheritance immediately and avoided even a one-year increase in the EFC. When I do pre-planning with families, I always ask if there is a possible inheritance. It's a natural tendency to avoid thinking about the death of a loved one; however, it is important to plan ahead. If there is any possibility of an inheritance, I recommend that the family put a plan in place to avoid losing even one dime of need-based assistance. The use of annuities, cash value life insurance, mortgage reduction, and combinations of the three need to be considered as a part of any pre-planning strategy. One plan might be to open an annuity. If the family receives an inheritance, they would put it directly into the annuity. Annuities generally do not count against need-based college financial aid. Furthermore, the appropriate annuity would provide access to the money. Depending on the family's situation, a cash-value life insurance policy might be a better option. There are also certain instances where it would be a good idea to use a portion of the inheritance to reduce the family's mortgage. The ideal plan depends on the family's financial situation.

Sometimes major life events can be even more difficult to anticipate than an inheritance, such as with changes in the economy. I have seen several families that had to change their financial plans due to the downturn of the economy. In several instances, families had planned to draw on their lines of home equity credit to finance college for two or three additional years. Then, the bank suddenly reduced the line of credit because of decreasing home values. Believe it or not, with proper planning, it's possible to avoid this type of problem. When a family decides to use their home equity to finance college, I generally advise them to refinance their mortgage and acquire the entire amount that they will need for four years. The family then shelters the money and draws upon those funds as college payments come due. This strategy has a number of advantages. First, the money is definitely available. Second, the decrease in home equity may reduce the expected family contribution and increase the opportunity of getting financial aid for the entire four years. Third, any funds that are left after four years can be used to pay down the mortgage. Alternatively, the funds might be left to grow in value.

Families have been affected by the economic downturn in other ways. Two of my clients had financial aid plans that made a lot of sense in 2007. The Griffith family had bought a pair of rental properties, which they had planned to sell just before their student entered college in 2009. By the end of 2008, it was obvious that this investment strategy was not going to work. The value of the rental properties had plummeted, making it a bad time to sell them. In fact, if they had sold the property according to their original plan, they would have suffered a loss. Since the Griffiths came to me after the housing market began falling out, we had to find another strategy for them. After discussing their options, the Griffiths decided to continue renting out the property. We selected colleges where their son would be an attractive candidate. In the end, he received a $12,000 per year academic scholarship, which kept the out-of-pocket costs low. The son took out student loans to pay the balance, and the parents will help him pay the loans back by selling the rental properties after the real estate market recovers.

In a similar case, the Hinson family had invested their college savings in stocks. When they came to see me in the fall of 2007, the time of their first college payment in 2009 was less than two years away. We discussed the risks of investing in stocks so close to the time of their first college payments. After reviewing their financial situation, I suggested that they allocate their assets into safer options. They placed their savings in conservative investments within a 529 plan. At the appropriate time, they stopped contributing to the 529 plan so that they had enough cash flow to supplement their savings with monthly payments. By the time college started, the Hinson family was able to cover their costs with payments from their 529 savings plan and their monthly cash flow. Of course, they are grateful that a large portion of their savings has remained sheltered from declines in the stock market. Some families have lost 50% of the value of their college savings because it was invested too aggressively. It is important to place your savings in increasingly conservative options as the time of the first college payment approaches.

Sometimes it's easy to anticipate a major life event, such as early retirement or having another child. A college financial aid consultant should help you prepare for the events that you know about. Other events, like changes in the economy, are more difficult to anticipate. An experienced consultant can help you anticipate the risks of common financial strategies and help you make plans to avoid mistakes.

Determine Your Expected Family Contribution

Once I understand a family's current financial situation, I enter the family's data into a software package that mirrors the FAFSA and the CSS Profile. I use the software to determine the Expected Family Contribution. The Expected Family Contribution (EFC) is the minimum amount that a family can be expected to pay for college. A family might be expected to pay more, but colleges and universities, will usually expect a family to pay at least the amount of the EFC when creating a financial aid package.

When it comes time to evaluate financial aid packages, a family should know their EFC. A college that expects your family to pay substantially more than the EFC has made a low financial aid offer. A college that expects a family to pay an amount somewhere near the EFC has made a good offer. An offer that provides substantially more financial aid than the EFC is an excellent offer. Excellent financial aid offers are typically reserved for exceptional students. This would be students who are in the top 25% of applicants at a particular college in terms of high school grades and college admissions tests. Your family can increase the chances of getting an excellent financial aid package by having the student apply to colleges where your student is an exceptional candidate.

It is a great benefit for a family to know the Expected Family Contribution several years before college starts. The EFC gives them a reasonable idea of how much they need to save for each year of college. Multiplying the number by four will give them a good estimate of how much money is needed for the entire four years. The more time that the family has to save towards this goal, the better off they will be.

There are Web sites with calculators that allow families to estimate their EFC for free. I have found these EFC calculators to be elementary at best. These calculators do provide a rough estimate of the EFC given the family's current situation. However, online calculators fall short of giving families the help they really need to know: how to effectively decrease their Expected Family Contribution. Once I have determined a family's initial EFC without doing any planning or reallocation of assets, I then run different scenarios for the family to find the best way of reducing their EFC, thereby maximizing financial aid eligibility.

Maximize Your Financial Aid Eligibility

A qualified college financial aid consultant will tell you not only what your current EFC is, but also how you can legally reduce your EFC. That is, the consultant will suggest ways of legally reallocating your finances so that they will not count toward the Expected Family Contribution. When you lower your Expected Family Contribution, you increase your eligibility for need-based financial aid.

Once I know a family's financial situation, I use my understanding of the EFC formula to run different scenarios. Then, I create a list of options for reducing the EFC. For instance, when a family has a portion of money invested in the student's name, I show the family the impact of reallocating the assets. Another example would be when a family has a second home that they use as a vacation home. I show them how much they could reduce their EFC by selling the home and placing the equity somewhere else. Let me give you an example of how the Blake family reduced their EFC. The Blake family had been investing money with a stock broker in a custodial account under the student's name. If the money had been kept there, it would have been reported on the FAFSA and, at the time, 35% of it would have counted toward the EFC. After consulting with me, the Blake family decided to apply for a life insurance policy for which the cash value does not get reported on the FAFSA. The family legally transferred the money from the custodial account to the life insurance policy. In the early years, the Blake family had all of the opportunities of the growth of the stock market. Then, before January of the student's junior year, the Blake family sheltered the money by moving it to the life insurance policy. By sheltering the money, the Blake family never had to report the funds and they reduced their Expected Family Contribution by about $15,000 per year!

When I present options for reducing the Expected Family Contribution, the family needs to bring their goals into consideration. For instance, if the parents are planning to sell their second home when they retire to provide extra income, then they might decide against selling it to fund a college education. One family I advised could have reduced their EFC by selling a second home. In the end, they decided against it because the parents were planning on moving into the second home and selling the first home when they retire. The financial benefits of any option need to be weighed against other family goals.

When the family has a significant amount of savings in the student's name, this is usually a primary target for reducing the EFC. While only 5.6 percent of the parents' assets contribute to the EFC, currently 20 percent of the student's assets go toward the EFC. By repositioning the student's assets, the family can often get a steep decrease in the EFC. Still, let me add a word of caution: not every family benefits from removing funds from the student's name. One family I assisted had heard during a high school financial aid night that it was bad to have money in the children's names. The husband had taken this advice to heart and moved his children's assets. By doing so, he had created a taxable event and had to pay income tax on the funds. When the family eventually came to me for assistance, the husband told me, "We've already moved all of our money out of the kids' names." During their pre-planning analysis, I found that moving the money did not help them at all. You see, even without considering the savings that were moved, the family's EFC was higher than the cost of college. Basically, the husband had needlessly paid a lot of money in taxes. His only accomplishment was to reduce his EFC from an incredibly enormous amount to an enormous amount. Since the final EFC was still higher than the cost of their student's college, moving the money had been a waste of effort and money. In addition, the way he moved the assets may have been considered illegal. And despite his efforts, his family would still be expected to pay the full cost of college. I wish the family had come to me earlier!

Please do not accept one-size-fits-all statements like, *"It is not good to have money in the children's name."* Every family's situation is different. A financial move that benefits one family may have little or no impact for another family. Furthermore, even if a move makes financial sense, it may not make sense given the family's other goals. Such was the case with the family that decided against selling their second home because they were planning to move into it during retirement. My job as a college financial aid consultant is to find out what options the family has for reducing the EFC to maximize financial aid eligibility. I then present those options to the family. It's then up to the family to decide which, if any, of the options make sense in their situation.

WARNING: BEWARE OF FALSE INFORMATION

ONE EXAMPLE OF A FALSE BELIEF:
Money in the student's name should be moved.

TRUTH: The decision to remove a student's name from assets should be based on the family's financial situation. Sometimes it makes sense and sometimes it does not. Moving assets can create a taxable event that may not lower the Expected Family Contribution at all.

Ensure that Major Risks are Covered

Let's imagine that a family has worked with a college financial aid consultant. The FAFSA has been completed and the student receives excellent financial aid. The parents are paying their share of the college costs and everything is going fine... until an unexpected accident happens and the breadwinner of the family passes away. Now what happens? If the family does not have major risks covered, then all of the college planning will be for nothing.

First of all, a family needs to have proper levels of life insurance. I have found that many families are underinsured. Some parents avoid getting life insurance because they feel uncomfortable planning for the possible death of a spouse. Other parents feel that it's a waste of money. I've even heard some people say that they don't want to make their spouse rich! At this point in your life, you need to set aside any discomfort you have about life insurance and consider what you would do if the wage earners in your family were to pass away. Life insurance salespeople have many formulas for determining the amount of coverage you should have. In my opinion, your life insurance should at least cover: the mortgage on your house, any loans and credit card debt, and the cost of college for all children in the family. My presumption is that this would give the spouse a clean slate and enable him or her to focus on providing for the family's daily needs, such as food, clothing, and utilities. If the spouse expects to have enough insurance to cover daily needs as well, then more insurance would be needed.

It is important for the breadwinner of the house to have disability income insurance as well. I follow the same rule of thumb here: disability income insurance should at least cover the family's mortgage, debts, and college costs.

What if you get in an auto accident or what if you get sued? Having the appropriate limits for auto insurance and homeowners insurance are extremely important. This is particularly true in places like New Jersey. In order to make auto insurance and homeowners insurance more affordable, New Jersey lowered the allowable limits for coverage. For instance, prior to March 1999, all New Jersey auto insurance policies had personal injury protection medical expense benefits of at least $250,000. Nowadays, a person can purchase auto insurance with as little as $15,000 of medical expense benefits. What happens if you get in an accident and you require more than $15,000 of medical care? Well, then you have to pay for it out of your pocket. It is well worth the extra cost of auto and homeowners insurance to select standard limits or higher. You do not want to put yourself or your family in debt due to inadequate coverage.

I do not personally sell auto and homeowners insurance. However, as I go through the pre-planning process with families, I look at their limits and encourage them to consider raising them if they seem low. This is especially important for families with teenage drivers. What if your student causes an accident and the family gets sued for a million dollars? You should ensure that your family has continued financial security in the event of a major accident.

POINTS TO REMEMBER

Chapter 3

Pre-Planning Analysis

- The main purpose of the pre-planning analysis is to help your family reduce your Expected Family Contribution.

- An assessment of the family's current financial situation includes the assets of the parents and the student.

- It is important to consider all of the family's financial goals and major life events. These can have an impact on whether or not to reallocate assets.

- The family should obtain an accurate estimate of their Expected Family Contribution and then consider the options they have for reducing it, which will increase their eligibility for financial aid.

- A family should get an accurate estimate of the Expected Family Contribution as early as possible. This will give the family time to save money for college.

- The family should be properly insured so that they are covered in the event that one of the parents unexpectedly passes away or becomes disabled.

Steps to Take Control

- Before meeting with the college financial aid consultant, the parents and the student should discuss the family's other financial goals. For instance, how many other children in the family will be going to college? When are the parents planning to retire?

- Collect your asset statements. Here is a list of the statements you will need.

INCOME STATEMENTS	▪ Latest federal tax return ▪ W-2 forms
INVESTMENT STATEMENTS	▪ Retirement investments (401k, 403B, pensions, annuities) ▪ Non-retirement investments (checking accounts, savings accounts, CDs, stocks, bonds, whole life insurance, etc.)
HOME & AUTO STATEMENTS	▪ Mortgage information for any houses ▪ Homeowner's policy declaration page for each house ▪ Auto policy declaration page

- Make an appointment with your college financial aid consultant to review your assets and do a pre-planning analysis.

Chapter 4

Financial Aid Forms

On the face of it, filling in financial aid applications sounds like it should be an easy task, right? It seems like you should just be able to get your financial statements, fill in the forms with the right numbers, and you're finished. From my experience, I find this to be far from the truth! In fact, when I began my business in 1997, about 90% of my customers came to me to help them get out of trouble from mistakes they made while trying to do the FAFSA themselves. A majority of them were the parents of high school seniors who had done little or no financial aid planning. I soon realized that I needed to work with the parents of sophomores and juniors to help them do the appropriate planning.

In this chapter, I'll give you're a brief overview of the most common financial aid forms. Then I'll describe the most common mistakes that people make when applying for financial aid. In the end, we'll look at what a college financial aid consultant can do to help.

Different Forms and Deadlines

To apply for financial aid, every college requires one or more of the following forms: FAFSA, CSS/Financial Aid PROFILE, and institutional forms.

1) FAFSA

FAFSA is the Free Application for Federal Student Aid. The United States Department of Education processes about 14 million of the applications each year. Based on information in the applications, the Department of Education disburses tens of billions of dollars in financial aid to college students. The key information collected on the FAFSA is the parents' income and assets, the student's income and assets, the ages of the parents, and the number of students attending college at the same time.

The FAFSA is the most widely used financial aid application in the United States. Although the FAFSA is designed by the federal government primarily for the purpose of identifying students eligible for federal financial aid, many financial institutions use FAFSA's calculation of the Expected Family Contribution to help determine other types of financial aid. Some colleges require all students applying for merit-based scholarships to submit the FAFSA. The reason for this is to ensure that applicants also take advantage of any need-based aid that they might qualify for. For instance, let's imagine that a student qualifies for a full tuition merit scholarship of $20,000 at a state college. If that student also qualified for $10,000 of need-based federal aid, then the merit-based scholarship might be reduced by $10,000, making that $10,000 of merit-based money available for other deserving applicants.

To get all the financial aid you deserve:

1) Do financial aid planning BEFORE submitting the FAFSA
2) Submit the FAFSA as early as possible
3) Provide consistent information on forms
4) Understand the perspective of college financial aid officers
5) Resolve any financial aid problems with the right people

The FAFSA can be completed as early as January 1 during the year of application. The deadlines set by each college should be used to determine the latest date of submission. However, the sooner that your application is submitted, the more likely you are to receive aid. This is because the federal government and most colleges distribute aid on a first-come first-served basis.

Some people mistakenly believe they should wait until they have completed their federal income taxes before submitting the FAFSA. This can be a costly error. First of all, college deadlines for the FAFSA can be as early as January 1, which is before many people receive their W-2 forms. Secondly, financial aid is usually distributed on a first-come first-served basis. It is best to enter estimated numbers and submit the FAFSA as early as possible. Once federal income tax forms have been filed, the revised numbers can be submitted. This is a common, expected part of the application process.

2) CSS/Financial Aid PROFILE

The CSS/Financial Aid PROFILE is administered by the College Board, the same organization that commissions the SAT Tests. Over 600 private colleges, universities, and scholarship programs use the financial information collected in the PROFILE to award nonfederal financial aid. The PROFILE asks more specific information about assets than the FAFSA. For instance, the PROFILE asks about home equity and may ask about such things as autos and home insurance, whereas the FAFSA does not.

Some private institutions require both the PROFILE and the FAFSA. It is very important to provide the exact same financial information on both the PROFILE and the FAFSA. Some institutions compare the information on the PROFILE and FAFSA to verify that the information is accurate. Forms with consistent information are processed immediately. Applications with inconsistent information are set aside while staff members make inquiries to determine the cause of the discrepancies. Such inquiries can become a costly waste of time, since financial aid is usually distributed on a first-come first-served basis.

Deadlines for the PROFILE often differ from FAFSA deadlines, especially if the student applies for early action or early decision. For early decision or early action applications, colleges may require the PROFILE as early as November 1 prior to the year of admission. Under such circumstances, the best strategy to use is to submit the same estimates on the PROFILE and the FAFSA. Corrections can be made later once federal tax forms have been submitted. If the college has already made a financial aid offer by the time the corrections are submitted, the college will simply adjust the award if necessary. This is a routine part of the financial aid process. Although it may seem unnecessarily tedious and time consuming to submit estimates and correct them later, it is an effective way to ensure that your family obtains all eligible financial aid.

3) Institutional Forms

Some colleges, universities, and scholarship funds prefer to use their own institutional forms instead of using the PROFILE service. The institutional forms may be required alone or in addition to the FAFSA. The same guidelines for submitting the FAFSA and PROFILE apply to institutional forms. First, use estimates to submit the forms as early as possible. Second, enter consistent estimates on all forms. Third, once you have filed your federal tax return, submit corrections. Following these three guidelines allows you to obtain all eligible financial aid by getting applications in early and avoiding delays from discrepant information. In addition, many institutional forms gather non-financial information about the family's background, place of worship, etc. in order to find qualified candidates for endowed scholarships.

Common Mistakes Made on Financial Aid Forms

In my experience as a college financial aid consultant, these are the most common mistakes that people make when filling out financial aid forms. While some of the mistakes may seem simpler than others, all of them bring the same consequence: loss of financial aid.

Mistake #1: Not Filling Out Financial Aid Forms

In the 1999-2000 academic year, half of all U.S. undergraduates, or 8 million students, failed to complete the FAFSA.[1] This is just incredible! For many people, the reason they don't apply is that they believe they earn too much to receive financial aid. Isn't it better to apply and find out whether you qualify than to make a wrong assumption?

Mistake #2: Failing to do Pre-planning

When I work with a family, we fill out a sample FAFSA and then identify ways of reducing the Expected Family Contribution before submitting the application. (I call this the Pre-planning Analysis, and I describe it in Chapter 3.) However, many families simply fill in the FAFSA and submit it without determining how they could reduce their Expected Family Contribution. This mistake is commonly made by Do-It-Yourselfers who don't think they need to consult with anyone to complete the form. Their problem is that they are potentially giving up thousands of dollars of financial aid by failing to reduce their Expected Family Contribution!

---

[1] King, J.E. (2004). Missed Opportunities: Students Who Do Not Apply for Financial Aid. *ACE Issue Brief*. Washington, D.C.: American Council on Education.

I find that Do-It-Yourselfers make two very common mistakes. First of all, they often keep too much money in the student's name instead of reallocating assets. This is a costly mistake. Let's consider a savings account with $50,000. If the money is in the student's name, then $10,000 is currently considered eligible for college expenses. If it's in a parent's name, then $2,800 is eligible for college expenses. If it's in a grandparent's name, then none of it is considered eligible. In this case, keeping the savings in student's name could reduce the family's financial aid by $10,000!

The second common mistake of Do-It-Yourselfers is to report assets incorrectly on the FAFSA. For example, let's say that a grandparent has saved $50,000 in a 529 education savings plan. Do-It-Yourselfers frequently report this on the FAFSA as the student's asset, when in fact it is the grandparent's asset and should not be reported. There goes another $10,000 in financial aid out the window!

Mistake #3: Missing Deadlines

Deadlines for the PROFILE can be as early as November 1st. The FAFSA can be due as early as January 1st. Some people think that they need to complete their federal tax forms before they complete financial aid applications, which is a big mistake! The key is to make estimates and submit the applications as early as possible. Corrections should be submitted after you've completed the federal tax forms.

Mistake #4: Entering Inconsistent Information

Some colleges require two financial aid applications. The most common combinations are the FAFSA together with the CSS Profile or the FAFSA plus an institutional form. Colleges often compare the information on these forms to ensure that it's accurate. When the information is inconsistent, then the forms are set aside and an inquiry is made to determine the reason for the discrepancy. Delays like this have actually prevented families from getting financial aid because their application sat waiting for an answer to a query while the funds were distributed to other eligible applicants. It is critical that the information entered on all financial aid forms be consistent.

Mistake #5: Entering Wrong Information

Entering the wrong social security number or address is just as bad as entering inconsistent financial information. If your application has wrong information, it will be set aside so that a query can be made while other applicants are receiving their aid awards.

Let me tell you what happened to one family that came to me for help. The husband had submitted the FAFSA for his twins. Jessica had received her financial aid award six weeks earlier, but Dawn had not received a reply. I learned from some simple research that Dawn's financial aid application was not accessible at the FAFSA site. When I followed up with FAFSA, I found that Dawn's application had been set aside for a query. As it turned out, the father had mistakenly entered the wrong birth date for Dawn. The application had been flagged for a discrepancy and set aside. The FAFSA processers will not let the applicant know what was entered incorrectly: the application just gets set aside until a correction is submitted. Thankfully, the fact that Jessica had received her award and Dawn had not received an award allowed the family to figure that something was wrong, and they took action. We were able to correct the problem and get Dawn the financial aid she deserved. If Jessica and Dawn had not been twins, the family might still be waiting to correct the issue.

How a College Financial Aid Consultant Can Help

I have many years of experience guiding families through the college financial aid process and helping people with their financial aid problems. That experience can help you take control of the college financial aid process in several crucial ways.

1) Take Control of Pre-planning

Why use money to pay for college when you could be saving it for retirement or using it to pay down your mortgage? Pre-planning is essential to getting the financial aid package that you deserve. A College Financial Aid Consultant will provide you with options for reducing your Expected Family Contribution, thus making you eligible for more financial aid. In some cases, such as reallocating funds that are currently in the student's name, it will be easy to make a decision. In other cases, such as the decision to keep or sell a car or a house, you will need to weigh your priorities. Still, it is better to make conscious decisions and develop a clear financial plan than to expose all your assets and surrender them to pay for college.

2) Take Control of Deadlines

Once the student has made the final decisions about where to apply for college, I ask the student to provide me with a list of selections. In addition, I ask for the type of application being submitted to each institution—regular, early action, or early decision. I then go to each college's Web site to determine the financial aid requirements and deadlines and create a schedule for submitting financial aid applications. Each year I submit the applications as early as possible to ensure that we meet all deadlines and obtain all eligible financial aid.

3) Provide Consistent Information

Once we have completed the pre-planning analysis and reallocated any funds, I sit with the family and put together the estimates needed for the financial aid forms. I enter the same information on all applications to ensure that they will be processed without delay. Once the family has submitted federal tax forms for the given year, I follow up on the original applications with revised information. I submit the revised information for the FAFSA, the PROFILE, and other applications on the same day to ensure that the colleges receive consistent information regarding the family's applications.

4) Understand the Perspective of College Financial Aid Officers

If you were to ask a college financial aid officer whether you should work with a consultant to complete the FAFSA, the officer would probably say that you should not. In fact, the officer would probably offer his or her own assistance. College financial aid officers tend to believe that they are the people to see about filling in financial aid forms properly. However, it is important to keep their perspective in mind. The goal of a college financial aid officer is to find out about your assets that can be used to pay for college. The financial officer will not help you make financial aid plans with your other goals in mind. So, a college financial officer will not say, "Oh, you should really move some of these assets out of your student's name so you can qualify for more financial aid." And I have never heard of a college financial aid officer saying, "The money that the grandparents set aside in the 529 plan is not a student asset. I corrected your FAFSA so that you would qualify for a better aid package." From the perspective of the college financial aid officer, 20% of any assets reported as student assets can be used to pay for college that year.

I do not mean to belittle college financial aid officers. They play an essential role at colleges. They are in charge of allocating the colleges' need-based awards fairly among a diverse group of applicants. They help make college affordable for students who qualify for financial aid. Still, I hope my point is clear: you cannot expect a college financial aid counselor to help you shelter assets for retirement or other worthy goals.

5) Work with FAFSA, College Financial Aid Officers, and Others to Resolve Problems

One skill that I have developed over the years is the ability to work with various people in the industry to resolve problems. Many families have come to me with situations in which colleges have mistakenly or unfairly reduced or withdrawn financial aid. In such instances, I am prepared to use my understanding of the system to work as an advocate for the family. I have gained experience at negotiating with college financial aid officers and FAFSA administrators, and I know how to use calm reasoning and well-prepared information to appeal unjust decisions.

Let me tell you about what happened to an engineering student at an Ivy League university. The student relied on her mother for financial support, and she was receiving need-based aid from the university up until the year after her mother became permanently disabled in a ski accident. At that time, the university completely removed her need-based aid. I helped the student write an appeal to the university regarding the decision to withdraw the need-based aid. The university turned down the appeal, so I organized a conference call among the student, the mother, the financial aid office, and me to see what could be done. There were a few reasons why the aid had been withdrawn. The main reasons were that the mother had received several sums of money during the year: a lump-sum settlement from the accident, as well as money from the sale of her house and her business. The mother was permanently disabled from the ski accident, so she was relying on the money for medical care and living expenses. However, the university had determined that this money could be used to pay for college and held it against the student for the purposes of financial aid. Technically, the university had the right to remove the aid; however, this money was intended for the mother's long-term care. In calm and clear terms, I said something like this: "The university is being very harsh here. You have a female engineering student with a 3.6 GPA, and you're taking all of her money away. Do you think down the road that she's going to give you any money toward your 5.8 billion dollar endowment? I don't think so. I am really disappointed in you as a university that you would actually take money away from a family whose mother has just become permanently disabled. Now, you could use your professional judgment in this special circumstance to do something good for the family, and your choice is not to do that? Am I right?"

The financial aid officer said that she could use her professional judgment as long as all of her questions were answered. I was then able to ask her what documentation could be provided that would allow the university to turn its decision around. The officer then proceeded to describe four types of official documentation that would be needed. Once the family had gathered and submitted the required information, the university did reverse its decision and reallocated the financial aid to the student.

For those families who seek my advice before submitting applications, I have consistently succeeded at helping them prioritize their goals and allocate their assets appropriately.

However, when a family needs help to resolve a problem, I am comfortable using my experience to negotiate a just resolution.

POINTS TO REMEMBER

Chapter 4

Financial Aid Forms

- Pre-planning is essential to getting the financial aid package that you deserve. Financial aid applications should be filled out only after the family has determined whether it is appropriate to adjust their assets to reduce the Expected Family Contribution. Families that fill in the FAFSA and other forms without pre-planning are potentially giving up thousands of dollars of financial aid.

- Do not expect a college financial aid counselor to give you advice on sheltering assets for retirement or other worthy goals.

- Forty percent of families who could have qualified for federal financial aid did not even fill out the FAFSA according to a recent national survey.

- It is critical that the information entered on all financial aid forms be consistent. Deadlines for the PROFILE can be as early as November 1st. The FAFSA can be due as early as January 1st.

- To meet financial aid application deadlines, it is best to enter estimated numbers and submit the applications as early as possible. Once federal income tax forms have been filed, revised numbers should be submitted. This is a common, expected part of the financial aid application process.

Steps to Take Control

- Parents should make an appointment with the college financial aid consultant to create the financial estimates that will be entered on the financial aid applications. These estimates should be made only after careful pre-planning and asset reallocation. The estimates should be made in September or October of the student's senior year in high school.

- In October of the senior year in high school, the student should provide the college financial aid consultant with a complete list of the colleges applied to, along with the type of application—regular, early action, or early decision.

- As soon as parents and the student have completed their federal tax returns, they should provide the college financial aid consultant with signed copies. This will allow the consultant to submit revisions to the financial aid applications.

Chapter 5

Comparing and Negotiating Financial Aid Offers

After all financial aid offers have arrived, the family needs to compile the information and compare the offers. The number that matters most is the out-of-pocket cost for the family. Once you have calculated the out-of-pocket cost for each college, it becomes easy to compare financial aid offers.

Next comes the biggest step of all: deciding which college the student will attend. The best situation is when the least expensive college is also the one that the student likes best. I wish that happened all the time! Unfortunately, the student's favorite college is usually more expensive than other choices. Sometimes, the family might even find that the student's favorite college is unaffordable. This is a heartbreaker! And it's one reason why it's helpful to go through the process with a college financial aid consultant. When I help families pick colleges, we avoid the unaffordable ones. And please note that the unaffordable ones are not always the ones with high tuition. The unaffordable colleges are those that have high tuition AND low levels of financial aid. Many parents make a big mistake by avoiding colleges with high tuition. Tuition is not the price tag! The price tag is the out-of-pocket cost for your family!

If it turns out that the student's favorite college is affordable, but it's slightly more expensive than some of the others, then the time has come to decide whether it's appropriate to negotiate for a better financial aid offer. Yes, it's sometimes possible to get more aid! If your student is the type of student that the college really wants, then it is possible to appeal for more aid and receive a better offer. The most important part is deciding whether it is reasonable to go back to the college and appeal for more aid.

In the first part of this chapter, I describe how to determine the out-of-pocket cost for a college. After that, I describe the process for comparing financial aid offers. The last part is about negotiating for a better financial aid offer. I provide guidance for deciding when it's appropriate to negotiate for a better offer, plus advice for negotiating successfully.

Calculating the Out-of-Pocket Cost

Some colleges try to estimate the out-of-pocket cost for you. Some of those estimates include the costs of books, supplies and living expenses, while others don't. And some colleges don't even try to estimate your out-of-pocket cost: they just send an award offer. If you try to compare several offers simply by looking at the financial aid letters, you'll get yourself frustrated in no time. The best way to compare financial aid offers is to make your own calculation of the out-of-pocket cost for each college. The following table shows how to find the out-of-pocket cost (see Figure 1).

Let me make a few points about what should and what should not be included in your calculations. It is important to include fees, books, supplies, and living expenses as part of the cost of attendance (COA). Supplies include costs such as a computer, a calculator, paper, a fan, and lamps for the dorm room. Living expenses include things like monthly phone bills, travel costs, and food outside of the meal plan. These are all college costs that will eventually need to be paid for, and all of them can potentially be covered by need-based aid if your family qualifies. Some colleges include books, supplies, and living expenses when providing a COA, while others just include tuition, room, board, and fees. To make a fair comparison of college costs, you should include estimates for books, supplies, and living in the COA for each college. Ignoring these expenses will lead to estimates that are 10% to 15% below the actual costs. In fact, many national

HOW TO CALCULATE THE OUT-OF-POCKET COST (Figure 1)

PROCESS	ABBREVIATIONS	SAMPLE CALCULATION FOR A COLLEGE
Find the total Cost of Attendance (COA), which includes: 1) Tuition, 2) Room & board, 3) Fees, 4) Books & supplies, and 5) Living expenses	COA	$35,000
Enter the Expected Family Contribution (EFC), which comes from the FAFSA.	-EFC	- $15,000
COA – EFC = NEED Subtract the EFC from the COA to get Need. The Need is the amount of financial aid that the family is eligible to receive.	Need	$20,000
Enter the financial aid Award. The Award includes all scholarships, grants, and loans.	- Award	- $12,000
NEED – AWARD = SHORTAGE/EXCESS Subtract the Award from the Need to get Shortage/Excess. A positive number indicates a Shortage, which is the amount of financial need that is not covered by the Award. A negative number shows Excess, which is the amount that the Award goes above your Need.	**Shortage** (When the number is positive) **OR** **Excess** (When the number is negative)	$8,000
Enter the Expected Family Contribution (EFC)	+EFC	+ $15,000
SHORTAGE + EFC = OUT-OF-POCKET COST Add the EFC from the Shortage to get the Out-of-Pocket Cost. This is the amount that the family needs to pay each year to send the student to this college.	Out-Of-Pocket-Cost	$23,000

publications actually publish the incorrect figures in their annual college comparisons.

Comparing Financial Aid Offers

When the time comes to compare financial aid offers, I find it best to create a spreadsheet that includes one column for each college. Creating a spreadsheet helps ensure that all the calculations for each college are made in the same way. Also, having the numbers for each college side by side allows for easy comparison. Here's a spreadsheet of costs for a student who applied to four colleges. (see Figure 2)

In the example provided on the spreadsheet, the student applied to two private colleges, one in-state public college, and one out-of-state public college. The second to last row provides the out-of-pocket cost for one year. This number was multiplied by four to get the out-of-pocket costs for the entire four years as shown in the bottom row.

Now let's do a little exercise. Look at the first row with the cost of attendance (COA). If we tried comparing costs using these figures, it looks as though the in-state public college is the least expensive. The out-of-state public college looks about $10,000 more expensive, and the two private colleges appear to be the most expensive. However, once we determine the out-of-pocket costs, we can see that the first private college is actually the least expensive for this family. In fact, it's slightly less expensive than the in-state public college. If the student's favorite college is private college 1, then the choice is easy: accept admission at private college 1.

You might find it surprising to see a private college with lower out-of-pocket costs than state colleges. Could this actually happen in real life? It could happen and it does happen! Let me give you two examples of students who found themselves

COST FOR A STUDENT WHO APPLIED TO FOUR COLLEGES (Figure 2)

	PRIVATE COLLEGE 1 (Student is in top 25% of applicants)	PRIVATE COLLEGE 2 (Student is in middle 50% of applicants)	IN-STATE PUBLIC COLLEGE (Student is in middle 50% of applicants)	OUT-OF-STATE PUBLIC COLLEGE (Student is in middle 50% of applicants)
COA	$45,000	$45,000	$25,000	$35,000
- EFC	$10,000	$10,000	$10,000	$10,000
Need	$35,000	$35,000	$15,000	$25,000
Award	$30,000 (86% of need)	$24,500 (70% of need)	$9,000 (60% of need)	$7,500 (30% of need)
Shortage	$5,000	$10,500	$6,000	$17,500
+ EFC	$10,000	$10,000	$10,000	$10,000
Out-of-Pocket (1 Year)	$15,000	$20,500	$16,000	$27,500
Out-of-Pocket (4 Year)	$60,000	$82,000	$64,000	$110,000

in a similar situation. One example is a young woman named Theresa, who applied to 17 colleges! Now believe me, I did NOT advise her to apply to 17 colleges. I did work with her to help her pick colleges, and she identified two schools that suited her well: a private university and an out-of-state public university. We also worked together to identify several other safety schools for her to apply to. Unfortunately, she listened to outside influences and she panicked, so instead of applying to 5 or 6 colleges, she applied to 17. She was accepted at 14, including her two top choices. When we sat down to compare out-of-pocket costs, I asked her which schools she absolutely did not want to attend. She selected six right away. We calculated the out-of-pocket costs for the other eight colleges. In the end, her two top choices provided the best offers. Here is a summary of the out-of-pocket costs for her two top choices:

	OUT-OF-STATE PUBLIC COLLEGE	PRIVATE COLLEGE
COA	$39,876	$50,100
- EFC	$7,356	$7,356
Need	$32,520	$42,744
Award	$28,516	$39,400
Shortage	$4,004	$3,344
+ EFC	$7,356	$7,356
Out-of-Pocket (1 Year)	$11,360	$10,700
Out-of-Pocket (4 Years)	$45,440	$42,800

When talking to others, Theresa had heard that her two top choices were too expensive, and she should look around and apply to less expensive colleges. She was surprised to find that her two top choices had provided the best financial aid offers. In fact, the in-state college she applied to cost more than her two top choices. She was even more surprised that the private college, which had the highest tuition of all her choices, ended up having the lowest out-of-pocket cost of all. Theresa would have been happy at either of her two top choices. After taking a second visit to each of the colleges, she decided to attend the private college.

Theresa made three mistakes: one, she listened to some poor advice; two, she panicked; and three, she applied to too many colleges. As a result, she spent more time and effort filling out applications than she needed to. Still, when it came time to decide which college to attend, she was in an ideal situation because her top choices had the lowest cost. Theresa was fortunate, but sometimes the student's top choice ends up costing more than other colleges that would also be a good fit. In this type of situation, the family needs to decide whether there are significant benefits to paying a higher cost for the student's top choice.

I can tell you about an instance when a young man named Roger was so emotionally tied to a certain college that he almost made his family pay a lot more money for college than they needed to. Basically, in addition to Roger's aspiration to earn a business degree, he wanted to have a big university experience where he could go to a football game each weekend and cheer for his team. Although Roger played on his high school football team, he knew that he didn't have the size or the talent to make it in college football, but he was still a big football fan. Ever since he was in junior high school he'd been rooting for the Green University football team, and he wanted to be a part of their long-time winning tradition. Even before visiting the campus, Roger had a sense of the Green University school spirit from televised football games. The cheering crowds, the blaring band, Green University crossing the line for another touchdown: Roger wanted to be a part of that scene. His visit to Green's campus and his walk through Green's massive, newly renovated sports stadium strengthened his desire to be a part of the Green Team. Before leaving campus, he bought a Green University football jersey, which he wore to high school to let everyone know where he was planning to go to college.

> *When comparing colleges, do not compare the cost of tuition. Tuition is not a price tag! The price to compare is the Out-Of-Pocket Cost for your family.*

When it came time for Roger and his family to compare out-of-pocket costs and decide where to go, they had to make a choice between two universities: Green University and Orange University. Green University had an out-of-pocket cost of $30,000 per year, while Orange University would cost the family $14,000 per year. Although Orange University cost a lot less, Roger had a hard time imagining himself going there. You see, one of Roger's friends had always rooted for the Orange University football team, and Roger could not see himself rooting for them. In fact, Orange University had been so low on Roger's list that he had not even taken the time to visit it. Despite the fact that the financial aid offers were so different, the two universities had very similar academic standards in the field of business. So when it came down to making a choice, I told Roger that I understood he had a real emotional reaction against Orange University, but it was in his family's best interest to consider going there. I persuaded him to visit the campus. I also reminded him that he was preparing to enter business, and that it would serve his family well to consider this from a business perspective. Was it really worth paying $16,000 more per year, which is $64,000 over four years, to get a degree from Green University instead of Orange University?

Roger did visit Orange University with his parents, and he enjoyed it. The visit allowed him to imagine himself attending Orange, and he could see that it would offer him the same type of experience as Green University at a much lower cost. Before he left the campus, he bought an orange football jersey, and he ended the rivalry with his friend by wearing the jersey to high school to show that he'd joined the orange side. When I last spoke to him, he was still a fervent fan of orange, and he was halfway towards earning his business degree.

Know when it is appropriate to negotiate

It is not always appropriate to negotiate for a better financial aid offer. If you have done everything right by applying to colleges where the student is an attractive candidate, negotiations will probably not be necessary. The applicants that the college wants will get the best financial aid offers right away. For instance, students with grades and standardized test scores that put them in the top twenty-five percent of applicants will get some of the best financial aid offers. Colleges also offer substantial financial aid packages to students who have other characteristics that appeal to them. Colleges that are working to maintain a strong school ochestra often award ample scholarships to talented candidates. Colleges with campus-wide volunteer programs that use student leaders often have large scholarships for students who have demonstrated leadership skills and eagerness to do volunteer work. When I help students decide where to apply, I look at their strengths and then I direct them to colleges that tend to offer good financial aid to students like them. As a result, there is usually no need to appeal for more financial aid.

Let's imagine that a student named Karen has gone through the steps that I recommend in this book. Let's imagine that she has chosen five colleges that fit her needs and budget. When she applied to the colleges, she highlighted her strengths. Her family has done pre-planning to maximize their eligibility for need-based aid and submitted financial aid applications on time. Then, let's imagine that her number one choice accepts her and offers a financial aid package that meets 102% of the family's need. In this situation, there is no need to negotiate because Karen's top pick has provided her with an ample financial aid award.

However, there are times when it's appropriate to appeal for more aid. Let's imagine that Karen's top pick offers her 80% of the family's need and her second choice offers her 100% of the family's need. If the two colleges have similar academic standards, then it would be worthwhile to approach her top pick and see whether the college would be willing to increase financial assistance to meet 100% of the family's need. There's nothing to lose by making an appeal. If Karen's appeal is successful and her top choice increases the financial aid offer to cover 100% of need, then Karen has an easy choice to make. If her appeal is unsuccessful, then the family needs to decide whether it is worth the extra cost to attend the top choice. If Karen has done a good job of selecting five colleges that meet her expectations, then she would probably decide to attend her second pick, where she'll have a satisfying college experience and earn a degree for significantly less money.

It is inappropriate to negotiate if the student's top choice has provided financial aid that meets 100% or more of the family's need. It would not make sense to go through the steps and waste everyone's time. However, if the student's top choice has not met 100% of the family's need, as determined by financial aid applications, then it would be reasonable to negotiate for a better financial aid package.

Don't annoy the financial aid officer

If you do find yourself in a situation where you need to negotiate, it is important to do it in the right way. The last thing that you want to do is make yourself a pain in the neck. College financial aid officers deal with a wide range of people every day, and they hear some of the same pleas for money again and again. Some of these pleas really annoy officers. Let me tell you two types of behavior that will surely turn them off.

The most irritating type of behavior is whining. Nothing gets under the skin of a college financial aid officer more than hearing parents complain that they do not have enough money. EVERYONE thinks that college costs too much. EVERYONE would like more financial aid. The worst thing a parent can do is earn $100,000 a year and claim to be poor, especially when financial aid officers deal with families who are earning $20,000 a year. Financial aid officers base their aid awards on documented information: information about the family's assets and information about the student's academic performance. Whining about how little you earn will do nothing to change the award. In fact, it's a sure way to irritate the officer and close off options that might be available to you. I am not saying that whining doesn't work. It can actually work quite well, but it does not make it any less irritating.

Demanding parents also annoy financial aid officers. Again, the financial awards are based on documented information about family income and student performance. It will not do any good to simply challenge the award by arguing that your student deserves more money. If your student has earned an award or achieved an honor that the college does not know about, it may be worthwhile to see if the college would increase their financial award in recognition of your student's achievement. You might be able to persuade the college to increase the award because you are providing documented information that the college is not aware of. However, simply arguing the point with a strong voice will earn nothing but a bad reputation in the office of financial aid.

It is important to understand that a college financial aid officer needs to meet federal and state guidelines when allocating funds. When an officer tells you that the college needs documents like pay stubs or tax forms, this is not negotiable. The officer needs to have required documents on file to show that the college is following regulations, just in case the college gets audited by the state or federal government. So, when a college financial aid officer says that a certain document is needed, this is not negotiable. Let me remind you of the engineering student at an Ivy League college whose aid was withdrawn after her mother was disabled in a skiing accident. In that case, the financial aid office needed four documents to show that the student did not have access to funds for the purpose of paying college expenses. In each instance, the college had a valid reason for requesting information. Once the family supplied the required documents, the college had the support it needed to continue allocating financial aid.

If a financial aid officer requests a certain document, you need to provide that document so that the office can provide your family with the financial aid you deserve.

Appeal to the officer with information

Since the financial aid packages are awarded based on documented information, you need to be ready to appeal by using such information. And you'll need to be ready with information about your family's financial need, the college's history of meeting financial need, and your student's strengths at that college.

Let's review how to calculate your family's financial need at a college. Need is determined by taking the cost of attendance at the college and subtracting the Expected Family Contribution, as determined by the FAFSA. An example is provided below.

COST OF ATTENDANCE – EXPECTED FAMILY CONTRIBUTION = NEED

$25,000 – $15,000 = $10,000

In this example, the annual cost of attendance is $25,000 and the Expected Family Contribution is $15,000. Since the cost of attendance is $10,000 greater than what the family is expected to pay, the family's need is $10,000. If the college meets 100% of the family's need, then the college would provide $10,000 of financial aid each year. This would probably come in the form of grants, loans, and work study opportunities.

Not all colleges have a history of meeting 100% of family need. Each college has a different history, but in general, private colleges tend to meet 80% to 100% of need, whereas public colleges usually meet only 30% to 60% of need. The lower cost of public colleges can sometimes compensate for the lower percentage of need-based aid, so the out-of-pocket cost for a public college is sometimes lower than the out-of-pocket cost for a private college. However, many families find that they can pay less for a private college than for their local state university.

But the main point here is that it is important to understand a college's financial aid history before negotiating for a better financial aid award. If you know that a college tends to meet 60% of a family's need, and your package covers only 30% of need, then you have a strong basis for an appeal. This is the type of information a parent can present to a financial aid officer with a reasonable expectation of getting a better offer.

In addition to understanding the college's financial aid history, it is also important to understand what makes your student attractive to the college. During the appeals process, it is important to highlight the student's strengths at that particular college. You'll want to consider the student's standardized test scores, grade point average, club and team activities, and background characteristics. Keep in mind that your student may have different strengths at different schools. For instance, an SAT score of 1200 would be a strength at a college where the average freshman earned a score between 1050 and 1150; however, it would not be a strength at a school where the average freshman earned a score of 1200 to 1300. Similarly, a student's participation on a high school soccer team that made it to the state playoffs might be a strength when applying to a college with a Division III soccer team, but it would not be an advantage at a college with a Division I soccer team. Likewise, having a minority background would be an advantage at a school that is not very diverse, but it would not be an advantage at a school that already has a diverse student population. During the appeal, you should focus on your student's strengths and avoid mentioning any weaknesses. If your student has a good standardized test score compared to other applicants and your student, who was editor of an award-winning high school newspaper, is interested in working on the college newspaper, then you should focus on those strengths.

Before making any appeal for additional financial aid, it is important to understand a college's record of providing need-based aid. First of all, you need to ensure that it is reasonable to make an appeal. If your student was offered a lower percentage than what is traditionally offered, then you will want to make this a key point of your request for additional aid. Furthermore, you need to reinforce the characteristics that make your student an appealing candidate. The officer who you speak with may not be familiar with your student's application. Letting the officer know about your student's strengths provides the officer with a positive incentive to offer additional aid.

Although each college has its own financial aid history, there are some general differences between negotiating for merit-based aid and need-based aid.

Negotiating for merit-based aid

The two main types of financial aid are need-based aid and merit-based aid. Need-based aid is determined through financial calculations that look at the cost of the college and the family's assets. On the other hand, merit-based aid is awarded based on the student's academic achievements. It is important to distinguish between need-based and merit-based aid because the type of documented support that you provide will be different. When appealing for more merit-based aid, it is necessary to provide documented information about academic achievements, such as standardized test scores or academic awards.

Some colleges are very rigid about their merit-based awards. Some even have tables on their websites that can be used to determine what the student's scholarship would be before submitting an application. By locating their grade point average (GPA) and standardized test score on the chart, students can see how much their merit-based award would be. In this type of system, there is room for negotiation if the student's academic performance improves after the application has been submitted. For instance, one student named Loretta submitted an application to a college with standardized test scores and a GPA that qualified her for a scholarship that covered one third of tuition. After submitting the application, she earned an even higher standardized test score. She called the financial aid office to let them know about the higher score, and the financial aid officer let her know that the score qualified her for an even larger scholarship. After the officer received official documentation of the test score, the college issued a letter increasing her merit-based award to half tuition!

Another situation when there is room for appeal is when the student has been offered a scholarship that has a range, and the student has not been awarded the highest amount. For instance, a student named Daniel earned a Trustee Scholarship at his college of choice based on his high grade point average and an excellent standardized test score. The range of the scholarship was from $4,500 to $10,000, and Daniel was awarded $5,000. During his senior year, Daniel won a prestigious award in a national competition. Daniel wrote a letter to the college, providing documentation of the award and appealing for more merit-based aid. Due to the high recognition of the award, the college increased the level of the Trustee Scholarship to the full amount of $10,000 per year.

Although colleges usually have strict standards for merit-based scholarships, it is appropriate to appeal for more merit-based aid when the student earns an academic achievement that is not included in the application. Two of the most common achievements are a higher standardized test score or a prestigious academic award. Since colleges need documented evidence of the award, I find that the most effective way to appeal for more merit-based aid is to write a letter and send it along with the documentation. Colleges are eager to attract students with high academic achievements, and they may grant additional merit-based aid for worthy accomplishments.

The family needs to consider carefully whether to make an appeal for additional merit-based aid. It would be a good idea to make an appeal if there is reason to believe that the student's top choice could offer a better scholarship. Maybe similar colleges have made better scholarship offers. Maybe the student's academic performance has improved since the application was submitted, or the student has earned an extraordinary honor that was not on the application. These are circumstances that would make an appeal worthwhile. Still, if a college that the student would enjoy attending has made an exceptional offer, then the reasonable thing to do is accept that offer and avoid the trouble of making appeals to other colleges.

Negotiating for need-based aid at public colleges

Now that we've looked at merit-based aid, let's consider need-based aid. Remember that need-based aid is determined through financial calculations that look at the cost of the college and the family's assets. When considering need-based aid, it is important to distinguish between public colleges and private colleges. Although there are exceptions to the rule, private colleges generally have more flexibility at increasing need-based aid.

When public colleges make their initial offers of need-based aid, they usually make the best offer they can. The need-based awards are determined from the information provided on financial aid applications and there is often no room for negotiation. One instance when it would be reasonable to appeal is when the college did not include a certain expense as part of the cost of attendance. For instance, let's say that the college requires all engineering students to have a laptop computer. Your student is going to be an engineering student, but the college has not included the computer as part of the cost of attendance. The family could appeal by requesting that the cost of a computer be added to the cost of attendance. This could then be used as a basis for negotiating an increase in the student's subsidized student loan. Another instance when it would be reasonable to appeal for more need-based aid would be if the family's financial situation has changed dramatically. The level of need-based aid depends in large part on the family's income as determined by the prior year's federal tax forms. If the family's income has gone down because a member of the family is no longer working or has changed jobs, then the family can appeal for more need-based aid. Of course, all changes need to be verified, so the family would need to provide necessary documents of any changes in employment and income.

Negotiating for need-based aid at private colleges

Compared to public colleges, private colleges generally have more flexibility at increasing need-based aid. In general, private colleges make low initial offers of need-based aid. Unlike public colleges, which tend to meet 30% to 60% of the family's need, private colleges tend to meet 80% to 100% of the family's need. This is a broad generalization to help you understand the typical situation. When working with any college, it is important to guide your expectations by understanding that particular college's history of awarding financial aid.

Let's look at an example to see the impact of a college's financial aid history. Based on the FAFSA, the Martins have an Expected Family Contribution of $16,000. This figure can be used to determine the Martins' financial need at each college where the student is applying, as shown in the following chart:

	PUBLIC COLLEGE	PRIVATE COLLEGE 1	PRIVATE COLLEGE 2
COST OF ATTENDANCE	$28,000	$46,000	$46,000
EXPECTED FAMILY CONTRIBUTION	$16,000	$16,000	$16,000
NEED	$12,000	$30,000	$30,000

The Martins' need at the public college is $12,000, whereas their need at the two private colleges is $30,000. Now let's look at the need-based aid that each college offers.

	PUBLIC COLLEGE	PRIVATE COLLEGE A	PRIVATE COLLEGE B
NEED	$12,000	$30,000	$30,000
NEED-BASED AID	$6,000 (50% of need)	$15,000 (50% of need)	$24,000 (80% of need)

The public college has offered need-based aid that covers 50% of the family's need. If the public college has a history of providing 50% of a family's need, it would be unreasonable to appeal for more need-based aid there. Let's look more closely at the offers from the private colleges. While Private College A has provided for 50% of the family's need with an offer of $15,000, Private College B has provided for 80% of their need with an offer of $24,000.

At this point, it is crucial to consider the history of providing financial aid at Private College A along with the student's preference. Let's say that both private colleges have a history of awarding 70% to 80% of a family's need. In that case, the Martins could make an appeal to Private College A, but there would be no basis for making an appeal to Private College B. At that point, the family needs to consider the student's preference. If the student prefers Private College B, then there is no need to make any appeals. The family is fortunate to get an offer for 80% of their need at Private College B. It would be a senseless effort to go to the Private College A to make an appeal when the student's top choice has already made a superior offer. It would be practical for the Martins to accept the offer of Private College B and avoid negotiations at Private College A.

However, let's consider the situation from a different perspective. Let's say that the student has a strong preference for Private College A. This would make it worthwhile for the Martins to appeal for more need-based aid. The Martins have no need to whine or be demanding; they have a solid basis of facts for their appeal. First of all, their student has selected the college as the first choice. At this point, it would be beneficial to mention the student's strengths and the reasons why the student has selected this college as the first choice. Secondly, the college has a history of providing for 70% to 80% of need, but the Martins were offered only 50% of their need. On top of that, Private College 2, which is quite similar to Private College 1, has provided an offer of $24,000, which meets 80% of the family's need. If the student is very enthusiastic about the college and would be willing to make donations in the future, it might be added that the student will certainly be a grateful alumnus in the future. Colleges want to accept students who are eager to attend and who are a good fit. A solid case like this would probably move the financial aid office to make another offer that would be closer to the 70% or 80% that is historically provided to first-year students.

To summarize, if a family does everything right to begin with, it should not be necessary to make an appeal for additional financial aid. If the student is in the top 25% of applicants and the college's programs meet the student's interests, then the college is a good fit and the student will probably be given the best possible offer right away. Before making an appeal, the family needs to consider carefully whether it would be beneficial. If the student has been provided a good financial aid offer at a college that is high on the student's list, then it may not be worthwhile to make an appeal. The family also needs to carefully consider whether the appeal would be reasonable. If the college has already made an offer that is consistent with the college's history of financial aid awards, then it is not reasonable to appeal. If you decide that it would be beneficial and reasonable to make an appeal, it is crucial to do it in the right way. Don't act whiny or demanding, or you could easily turn off the financial aid officer. It is important to present the facts of the matter to show your student is a good fit with the college, and similar students have received better offers. Focus on information that will make your student sound attractive to the financial aid officer. Focus on the information that would compel a reasonable person to increase the financial aid offer.

POINTS TO REMEMBER

Chapter 5

Comparing and Negotiating Financial Aid Offers

- If the student is in the top 25% of applicants and the student's interests fit well with the college's programs, then the college will make a good financial aid offer from the beginning. In this case, no appeal for additional financial aid is necessary. It is better to get a good initial offer than to find that you need to appeal.

- When deciding whether to make an appeal for more need-based aid, the family needs to consider whether the college's offer is satisfactory by looking at the college's history for need-based aid. If the college has a history of covering 70% of need and the family has been offered 60% of their need, the family has a reason to make an appeal.

- When deciding to make an appeal for more merit-based aid, the family needs to consider how strong the student is compared to other applicants. If the student is among the top 25% of applicants and the college has not made a good merit-based offer, then the family has a reason to appeal.

- If you do make an appeal, do not irritate a college financial aid officer by whining or acting demanding.

- When making an appeal, focus on the student's strengths.

- Private colleges generally have more flexibility in negotiating need-based aid than public colleges. The chance of negotiating for better merit-based aid at private and public colleges is generally the same. Still, individual colleges vary greatly, and it is important to know the financial aid history of the colleges where your student is applying.

- College financial aid officers need to meet federal and state guidelines when allocating funds. When an officer tells you that the college needs documents, this is not negotiable.

Steps to Take Control

- To increase the chances of getting a good financial aid offer from the beginning, apply to colleges where your student is in the top 25% of applicants.

- Do financial aid pre-planning with your college financial aid consultant to determine if your family will qualify for need-based aid. If your family qualifies, it is important to apply to colleges that award high percentages of need-based aid. Use college guides to find each college's history of providing need-based aid.

- Do research to find out what merit-based scholarships your student qualifies for at each college. Some colleges provide a chart that uses the student's standardized test scores and grade point average. Others have a series of scholarships that provide different amounts of money according to the student's academic performance.

- As soon as the student has received all financial aid offers, meet with your college financial aid consultant to discuss the offers. The consultant will help you make a final selection and determine whether any negotiations are necessary.

Chapter 6

Make a Personal How-to-Pay Plan

The goal of the personal how-to-pay plan is to figure out how your family can pay for a full college education for all students in the family. I cannot overstate the importance of making a how-to-pay plan for the full four years of college. The worst thing that can happen is to make a short-sighted plan that covers only one or two years, which then forces the student to drop out when money is no longer available. You want your child to complete all four years of college, don't you? And you want your first AND your last child to go to college, right? Of course! Well then, the payment plan should cover the full scope of your goal: it should cover all four years of college for each and every child.

Every single family is in a different financial situation. No two plans are the same because each plan needs to suit the situation of a specific family. However, every family has only four ways to pay for college:

- **With cash flow**
- **With savings**
- **With cash flow + savings**
- **With cash flow +savings + loans**

Let's look at the features of each payment method. For each one, let's consider the Morgan family. The Morgans have a student who needs to pay $24,000 per year, which is $96,000 over the course of four years.

Cash Flow

Paying by cash flow would work if the Morgan family had

$2,000 of income per month that they could devote toward college. Now, even if this is an option that works for the Morgans, it may not be the BEST option for them. This is because the Morgans have to pay taxes on all of the cash they use to pay for college. So, in order to get $24,000 per year to pay for college, the Morgans actually have to earn about $40,000 when you add on the $16,000 that is being paid in taxes. In effect, if the Morgans pay with cash, they are spending about $40,000 each year to pay a bill of $24,000.

If the Morgans were able to pay for college with cash, I would help them explore other options that would reduce their tax burden. Even though they might be able to pay with cash flow, there might be other options that have a better tax advantage. For instance, the Morgans might qualify for a low-interest home equity loan that they could use to pay for college. In that case, the potential tax deduction would be greater than the interest, and the overall yearly payment would be less than the $40,000 they would pay with cash. A home equity loan is just one of several tax advantaged options they might consider.

Savings

There are two important considerations when managing college savings:

1) **Consider college costs for ALL children.**

2) **Investments should become more conservative as high school graduation approaches.**

When making a college payment plan, it's important to consider ALL children in the family. Let's imagine that the Morgans have $96,000 in savings for college. If they have only one child, then this will be enough to cover their college costs.

But what if they have two children: one who is entering college this year and another who is entering college two years later? The savings will be depleted after three years. If the Morgans have two children, their savings are not enough to allow both children to graduate with college degrees. They'll need to develop a different plan.

The family's payment plan should cover all four years of college.

It's also very important to make savings investments more conservative as students approach college age. As time passes, the investment portfolio should move from equities to avoid any losses from drops in the market. You may have heard this type of advice when investing retirement funds. However, there are important differences between retirement funds and college funds. College should be only four years per child. Most families I work with have to think about funding eight years worth of college for two children. On the other hand, retirement funds usually need to last anywhere from 14 to 24 years, depending on life expectancy. If you get too conservative too early with retirement funds, you lose value in your investments because of inflation. So even though investors become more conservative with their retirement funds as they near retirement, they still keep a substantial portion in stocks so that their investment does not lose value to inflation.

College funds should be invested more conservatively than retirement funds. I recommend having the entire savings in guaranteed investments by the time of the junior year. This protects the savings from unexpected dips in the market and ensures that the money is available when tuition is due. Unfortunately, a number of my clients came to me after it was too late to hear this advice. One family had about $100,000 invested in a 529 Plan at the beginning of 2008, and the entire savings was in equities. By the time they came to see me in 2009, the value of the account had dropped by about 40% to about $60,000. Their student is in the senior year of high school, and it is unlikely that the investments will regain their value by the time the money is needed to pay college costs. Instead of having money to pay for four years of college, the family now has enough to pay for about two and a half years. They have revised their plan to cover the entire four years. Luckily, the family has assets that will allow them to retain some of their college savings, giving it more time to recover its value.

As always, it is important to begin saving early for college costs. In addition, the family needs to consider college costs for all children and adjust the investment to make it more conservative as time passes.

Cash Flow + Savings

Let's go back to the example of the Morgan family and let's say that they have one daughter. If the family has some savings and they can pay the remainder with cash, then they can use a combination of cash flow and savings to pay for college. If they needed $96,000 to pay for four years, then this plan would work if they had $48,000 in savings plus $1,000 per month in cash flow during the course of four years.

Still, even if the Morgans can pay for college with a combination of cash flow plus savings, it might not be the best option. Other options might allow the family better tax advantages. In addition, certain options may allow the family to retain some of their savings.

It is always important for a family to consider all of their long-term goals. I like to have people consider their savings goals by talking about piggy banks. In the case of the Morgan family, they have three piggy banks they need to be concerned with: one for college, one for the daughter's wedding, and one for the parents' retirement. The wedding would probably be the smallest piggy bank. The middle one, which is going to require a greater investment, is going to be college. The retirement piggy bank is the biggest one, and any funds that are already there should not be touched for any other purpose. Any how-to-pay plan should ensure that the Morgans can devote funds for each of these three goals.

I always encourage families to consider all of the options that are available to them. It might be possible for the Morgans to devote a majority of their savings and cash flow to college costs. However, if that plan prevents them from saving money for their daughter's wedding or retirement, then it is probably not the best plan. Before determining whether cash flow + savings is the best option, it is important to consider the possibility of using cash flow + savings + loans. More specifically, it is important to consider the option of using student loans to cover part of the college costs.

Cash Flow + Savings + Loans

Maybe the Morgans do not have enough cash flow and savings to pay for college. Or maybe they do have enough cash flow and savings, but they want to devote some of the cash flow and savings to another purpose. Or maybe the value of their savings investments has declined, and they want to give the savings time to bounce back. As long as they qualify for a loan, then paying with cash flow plus savings plus loans becomes an option.

Some parents are reluctant to have their student take on loans before getting a job. I like to remind parents that when students pay for part of their education, they are likely to take their studies more seriously. Furthermore, college presents the student with two opportunities: access to guaranteed student loans, as well as the chance to build a positive credit record.

There are a wide variety of loans available, and it is important for your family to understand what is available, as well as their features. I have to stress the importance of comparing all of the options and then selecting the option that is right for your family. I realize that it is difficult to consider all of the choices and select the option that is best, but this is one area where the advice of a college financial aid consultant can make a big difference.

Generally, there are three types of college loans: federal, state, and private loans. Every family has a different financial situation. Every family should consider all of their options to decide whether loans are a good option and, if so, to select the type of loan that is best for them.

Federal Loans

There are two types of federal loans: student and parent loans. Students qualify for federal student loans by filling out the FAFSA form; qualification does not depend on the parent's income or credit rating. Federal student loans are placed in the student's name. When the federal student loan is subsidized, the federal government pays the interest on the loan until six months after the student has left college (whether the student has graduated or dropped out). After being out of college for six months, the student needs to begin paying interest and principal on the loan. When the federal student loan is unsubsidized, the student will find that interest on the loan will accrue from the very beginning.

The second kind of federal loan is the parent loan called the PLUS loan. Should parents need to apply for PLUS loans, they need to have adequate assets and credit ratings to qualify. The loan is in the name of one of the parents, and payments on principal and interest need to be made from the beginning. The best feature of a PLUS loan is that it is a 10-year loan and it is forgiven if the parent dies or becomes permanently disabled. That is, if the parent who qualified for the loan passes away or becomes permanently disabled, the loan will not transfer to the spouse or the student.

The student subsidized loans are the best deal of all the federal loans. Since the federal government pays interest on the loan while the student is in college, it's basically an interest-free loan for that time. Even if a family has other means to pay for college, it is often beneficial to take advantage of the federal subsidized loans. Savings and investments can grow elsewhere for several years and be used to pay the balance of the loan once the student has graduated.

State Loans

Depending on the state you live in, state loans may or may not be available. The features of state loans vary from state to state and from year to year, but they are generally a good deal. State loans usually have low interest rates and a long payment term, such as fifteen or twenty years. In addition, some states have options that allow you to choose whether you will begin paying interest and principal right away or pay interest only until the student leaves college.

Private Loans

Private loans can be divided into two different types: loans from institutions and personal loans. The loans from institutions all require appropriate assets and credit scores to qualify, and all require payment from the onset of the loan. The most common sources of private institutional loans are local banks, credit unions, national banks, and companies such as Sallie Mae and Nelnet. The benefit of these institutions is that they are ready sources of funds for qualified borrowers. The drawback is that loans offered by these institutions usually have variable interest rates and may have high interest caps as opposed to the fixed rates that are usually available with federal or state loans.

Personal loans can have great advantages or disadvantages, depending on the family's situation and the terms of the loan. The three types of personal loans that I often discuss with families are loans from retirement accounts, loans from rich relatives, and home equity loans. When I talk about loans from retirement accounts, I am usually trying to persuade families not to use them. Borrowing from retirement should be avoided at all costs! Why shouldn't you borrow from your retirement account? The answer is simple: you cannot borrow for retirement, but there are many other sources of college finances. For instance, the family could get a loan from another source, the student could register for ROTC, or the student could reduce costs by starting at community college. As a responsible parent, you need to ensure that you save enough for retirement so that you do not need to rely on your children for financial assistance. Since you cannot borrow to pay for living expenses in retirement, it is important to leave retirement funds alone . . . until retirement! I have been working as a college financial aid consultant for many years. I've assisted over 1,000 clients, yet I've encountered only TWO situations when using retirement savings has turned out to be the best option. In those two instances, the how-to-pay plan put the parents in a better position for retirement after paying for college. Believe me, these were two extremely rare situations. The vast majority of families should leave that piggy bank alone!

If you have rich relatives, borrowing from them is a good idea if they are willing to lend a sufficient amount of money at a low interest rate. So, let's say that a grandparent has a sufficient amount in a CD that's earning less than two percent interest. You could offer to pay four percent, which is lower than even federal and state loans. If the grandparent agrees to your offer, it's a good idea to write up a contract and sign it for the security of everyone concerned.

Home equity loans are a good alternative in the right situation. If the family has enough equity in their house, they will be able to get a loan at a good interest rate. At the same time, the debtor may get a tax deduction on interest payments. However, the family needs to be sure that they have enough cash flow to cover the equity loan payments, otherwise, they will be putting the house at risk. About 20% of the families I work with find that using a home equity loan together with cash flow is the best option to pay for college. This is the best option for these families because once they have paid for college, they have the option of paying off their mortgage in less time than they were originally scheduled to. For example, let's take a family that has 17 years left on a 30-year fixed mortgage at 6.0%. They have two children who they have to put through college over a period of six years. Their out-of-pocket cost is $20,000 per year. After reviewing all of their options, we found that using funds from refinancing the house plus cash flow was the best option. Basically, we refinanced the house and put the cash they obtained from the refinance into a guaranteed savings vehicle. Using that fund, the parents paid for all six years of college. Once college was paid for, the parents were able to use the remainder of the fund to pay off their mortgage in year 14 instead of year 17. Of course, the parents did not have to use the money to pay off the mortgage. The cash was available to do whatever they wanted to do. They could have just as easily allocated the cash towards retirement or taken a cruise. The important step they made was that they did NOT take additional loans on their home equity each semester, which would have created larger and larger payments as their children went through college. Instead, they obtained all the funds they needed by refinancing their house, and then they sheltered those funds. By paying for college with the sheltered funds and by paying the refinanced mortgage with their cash flow, the family was able to pay for college and then pay off their house three years early!

Using home equity can be a good way to get a low-interest loan on a tax-favored basis, but the family needs to make sure that they are not putting their house at risk. First of all, the family needs to use the home equity properly, and they need to ensure that they have the cash flow to continue making payments. In my experience, I find that families tend to use home equity lines of credit without realizing that they have better options. Although many families do use home equity lines of credit, that does not make it the best option. The main problem is that the home equity payments keep getting larger as the semesters pass, and families sometimes find that they don't have enough money to continue making these payments before the student has graduated. Let me give you an example of one family who recently came to me for advice. The family has two students: one of them has finished college and one is in the junior year. The parents have been paying for college with their home equity line of credit. The father has just lost his job. Since the family has already used up their cash and their home equity line of credit on college costs, they have no savings to turn to, and they're going to lose their house. If the family had come to me earlier, I would have advised them not to use their home equity in the way that they did. I would have also advised them to take advantage of state or federal loans, which would have eased the burden on their cash flow. In addition, payments on the state or federal loans could have been deferred while the father was out of work. For this family, using their home equity to finance college seemed like a good idea at the time. It was certainly possible: the banks let them do it. However, a different how-to-pay plan would have preserved a portion of their home equity in an investment and kept their monthly mortgage payments lower, making it more likely that the family could have kept their house when the father lost his job.

The purpose of the how-to-pay plan is to help the family find a way to pay for four-years of college for all of the students in the family. It is crucial to consider ALL of the students and to create a plan that will cover every year of college. Failure to do so can force a student to drop out. Another important consideration when making a how-to-pay plan is to find the most tax-favored way of paying for college. When you add on the associated taxes, using $25,000 in cash to pay for college is like paying $40,000 for a $25,000 bill. Using a tax-favored option will allow the family to devote more of their income to other important financial goals.

POINTS TO REMEMBER

Chapter 6

Make a Personal How-to-Pay Plan

- The purpose of the how-to-pay plan is to help the family find a way to pay for four years of college for each of the students in the family.

- It is crucial to consider ALL of the students and to create a plan that will cover every year of college. Failure to do so can force a student to drop out.

- Every family has only four ways to pay for college:
  - **With cash flow**
  - **With savings**
  - **With cash flow + savings**
  - **With cash flow +savings + loans**

- Even if a family can pay for college with some combination of cash flow and savings, this may not be the best option. There are often more tax-advantaged options that will save the family money.

- Federal and state loans usually have fixed interest rates, while private loans often offer variable rates.

- A home equity loan can be a good alternative, as long as the house is not put at risk.

- If you secure a loan from a rich relative, sign a contract to preserve the peace of mind for all people involved.

- Avoid borrowing money from retirement accounts unless you have considered all other options and decided that this is the best option for you.

Steps to Take Control

- First of all, do pre-planning to consider all of your payment options. If you are not sure whether you have considered all your options, then make an appointment with a college financial aid consultant.

- During financial pre-planning, let your college financial aid consultant know about all of your assets and income, as well as your financial goals.

- When deciding where to apply, work with the college financial aid consultant to ensure that you select colleges that are within your family's means.

- As soon as you have received all of your financial aid offers, work with the college financial aid consultant to weigh the offers in terms of the student's preference and the cost of attendance.

- As soon as you have decided which college to attend, work with the college financial aid consultant to discuss options for your how-to-pay plan. The consultant will present tax-favored options that will help the family retain savings and cash flow for other financial goals.

Chapter 7

False Information from Surprising Sources

FAFSA forms contain the following warning:

WARNING!

BE WARY OF ORGANIZATIONS THAT CHARGE A FEE
TO SUBMIT YOUR APPLICATION OR TO FIND YOU MONEY FOR COLLEGE.
IN GENERAL, THE HELP YOU PAY FOR CAN BE OBTAINED FOR FREE
FROM YOUR COLLEGE OR FROM FEDERAL STUDENT AID.

I agree that the answers to many college financial aid questions can be obtained for free. You can easily get answers to questions like "Where can I get the FAFSA forms?" or "How can I submit them?" However, it's hard to find good advice about the difficult questions. Try calling a college or Federal Student Aid to ask these questions:

1) *Which colleges are likely to offer my student good financial aid packages?*

2) *Is it a good idea for me to use home equity to pay for college?*

3) *What is the most tax advantaged way for my family to pay for college?*

It's hard to get good advice about the choices that a family should make. Neither college financial aid officers nor Federal Student Aid representatives are going to understand your family's financial situation well enough to offer the best advice.

As a college financial aid consultant, my job is to understand each family's unique situation. I then use that information to help the family pick colleges that meet their academic goals and their financial plans. I also help families find ways to pay for college that allow them to meet their other financial goals at the same time.

I do understand the reason for the FAFSA warning. There are businesses that charge money for services that could have been obtained for free. The main problem is that there is currently no federally recognized system for certifying genuine college financial aid consultants. The profession is relatively new, and several organizations in the United States are competing to become the definitive governing body. Some day in the future, college financial aid consultants will have a single governing body and clear rules that regulate their activity. It will be easy to know whether a college financial aid consultant is certified, in the same way that it is easy to know whether an accountant is certified. For now, it can be difficult to sort out the people who are out to make a fast buck from those who can provide clear, in-depth guidance to your family. So how do you decide whether someone is qualified to help you? One way would be to ask the individual these five questions:

1) *How can I lower my Expected Family Contribution and maximize my eligibility for financial aid?*

2) *How do I pick schools that will give me the best financial aid package?*

3) *When filling out the FAFSA and CSS Profile forms, what common mistakes should I avoid?*

4) *Once colleges have financial aid offers, when is it appropriate to negotiate for a better package? How do I negotiate?*

5) *How can I pay for college and still devote money to other important goals, like saving for retirement?*

Any person who advises you should be able to give you satisfactory answers to each of those questions. Their answers should be in line with the information that I have provided in this book, as well as the sample answers provided in the *Steps to Take Control* at the end of this chapter. In addition, the consultant should be able to give you a description of how s/he can help your family. I find that each family has different needs, and some families need more help in certain areas than others. Personally, I offer each family a free consultation at my office or on a conference call. After learning the basic information about the family's goals and current situation, I let the family know the areas where I can help them, along with the cost of my services. At that point, the family is free to go home and discuss whether they require my services. It is a basic principle that people need to know what they are paying for. I discourage you from using any service that requires payment of a fee before you meet with the consultant and learn the specific services that are provided.

High school guidance departments are in the same situation as individuals: they aren't sure where to turn to for advice about college financial aid. Most high schools organize an event called college night or financial aid night for the parents of college-bound students. You would think that college night would be a good source of information. Think again! Since guidance counselors are not experts in college financial aid, the guidance office usually invites a guest speaker, who is usually a college financial aid officer from a nearby college. I have attended several presentations like this, and each time I was disappointed by the amount of wrong information provided at these events. In each case, the speaker was an honest, well-meaning college financial aid officer who did not have the breadth of knowledge to answer all of the parent's questions. Let me give you one example of a high school financial aid night that I went to recently. The speaker was the director of admissions and financial aid at a local state college. Here's a summary of the main points that he provided during his 75-minute presentation:

- The speaker immediately acknowledged that he was not a financial aid planner, but stated that he understood the financial aid industry. It was quite clear that he was not a financial aid planner when he related his experience of sending his daughter to college and stated, "I was shocked when I got the bill."

- He provided examples of college costs. Community college is about $10,000 a year, the state college where he works is about $20,000 per year, and a local private university is about $52,000 per year. These numbers were selected to put the college where he works in the best light. He considered the cost of college to be the price for tuition, room, and board. He never discussed the importance of calculating the family's out-of-pocket cost. Of course, he never mentioned that many families can send a student to a private college for the same out-of-pocket cost as a state college.

- He liked state education loans better than PLUS loans, but he could not say why. However, his biography showed that he had been the head of the state agency overseeing the state loan program.

- When discussing merit-based aid, he provided information about the scholarships that were available at the state college where he works. This was not relevant to people who were applying to other colleges.

- The speaker spent at least ten minutes discussing the FAFSA. As a member of the audience, I expected to hear legal steps that could be taken to maximize qualification for financial aid. Instead, the speaker blamed parents for providing incorrect information on the FAFSA. He gave examples of some common mistakes and said that the process is difficult because parents play games. He emphasized that the financial aid office is error free and that they represent the federal government. Parents just need to give them the information they need, and the financial aid office will determine what the family can afford to pay. He did not impress me as a person who would help me maximize financial aid.

- He stated that college financial aid officers do not negotiate.

- Throughout his presentation, he never mentioned the CSS Profile, which is used by many private colleges to determine need-based aid. He probably ignored the CSS Profile because it is not required at state colleges. But this was supposed to be college night, where parents learn general information about applying to any college.

At the end of the presentation, the speaker answered nine questions from the audience. He answered four of them incorrectly. Fifty six percent correct is not a very good percentage for an expert! What bothers me more is that if parents believed the incorrect information, it will cost their families tens of thousands of dollars. Here's a summary of the questions and their answers.

Questions Answered Correctly

1) *Can you estimate on the FAFSA?*

Answer: Yes, you should make the best estimate that you can. Don't wait until you have completed your tax returns.

2) *If you fill out the FAFSA, and then your income decreases, what happens?*

Answer: Financial aid officers can make changes based on unemployment, divorce, flood, fire, disability, and other unusual circumstances.

3) *Why do colleges ask whether you are applying for aid on the admissions application?*

Answer: This is for budgetary reasons. It is best to be honest.

4) *If 1,000 applicants are accepted and get financial aid offers, but only 300 attend, what happens to all of the other money?*

Answer: We don't get any money back. We estimate ahead of time that only 30% are going to attend.

5) *How does the money in a 529 plan count against you for financial aid?*

Answer: Put an aunt or uncle as the owner, so that it is not counted as either the parent's or the student's asset. The speaker did not get specific about why this is the case. If the 529 plan is in the student's name, the family will be expected to contribute 20% of its value towards college costs each year. If the 529 plan is in a parent's name, the parent will be expected to contribute 5.6% of its value towards college costs each year. If the plan is in a grandparent's name or an aunt or uncle's name, then none of its value counts against the family when calculating financial aid.

Questions Answered Incorrectly

6) *If someone bought savings bonds for my student, do they need to be reported as a student asset on the FAFSA?*

<u>Answer:</u> The speaker stated that they do need to be reported as a student asset. This is incorrect. According to FAFSA, if there are two names on the bond, it can be listed either way. If the parent bought the savings bonds for the student, the bonds could be listed as either the parent's asset or the student's. (It would be to the family's advantage to list it as the parent's asset.) If a grandparent bought the savings bonds, then the bonds would not need to be included on the FAFSA at all.

7) *Will I have to worry about getting a large amount of aid in the first year, and then not getting as much in the following years?*

<u>Answer:</u> The speaker incorrectly stated that private colleges have a tendency of doing this, and that this is less likely to happen at a public college. However, in my experience the chances that aid will fall are equal at state and private colleges. The key to maintaining current levels of aid is to do financial aid planning to ensure that you report similar levels of assets on the FAFSA or CSS Profile each year.

8) *How many schools can you put on the FAFSA?*

<u>Answer:</u> The speaker incorrectly stated that five or six colleges could go on the FAFSA. Years ago it was true that the maximum number was six colleges at a time. However, for several years now the maximum number has been ten colleges at a time. Special

procedures need to be followed if a student applies to more than ten colleges. There is no limit to the number of colleges that can receive FAFSA information.

9) *My son would like to go to college in another country. How does that fit in with the FAFSA?*

Answer: The speaker incorrectly stated that the FAFSA does not apply. However, I regularly work with students who want to go to college in Canada, countries in Europe or elsewhere. The system works the same as if they were attending college in the United States, and many students are able to qualify for federal financial aid, including student loans. Citizens of the United States qualify for U.S. federal financial aid when they study abroad for a semester, and even when they apply directly for admission to a university in another country.

This is just one example of the type of false information that gets spread by "experts" at college night. I wish I could say that this was an exceptionally bad presentation, but it wasn't. I've been to several presentations given by college financial aid officers, and two symptoms are common: they tend to focus on information about their own college, and they provide inaccurate information about FAFSA regulations.

Another common problem with college night presentations is that the information often comes too late. For example, the college night that I just discussed was held in January for the families of juniors and seniors. Juniors were led to one room to discuss college admissions, while seniors attended the presentation about financial aid. This is far too late for the families to do any financial planning in preparation for the FAFSA. For instance, imagine that you are the parent of a senior and you just learned that it's better to put your 529 plan in the name of an aunt, uncle, or grandparent. That's great information, but it's too late to do anything about it! Remember that financial aid planning should be completed prior to January 1 of the junior year. The high schools would be heroic if they changed their event calendar to highlight this fact!

> *Don't rely on your high school's college night to answer your questions. The "experts" don't always have the right answers!*

Sophomores and their parents should get general information about the admissions process and start visiting colleges. By the end of the junior year, students should know where they're going to apply. Sophomores and their parents should also get information about the financial aid process, the FAFSA, and the CSS Profile. It is best to start financial aid planning in the sophomore year at the latest. If the family needs to reallocate any assets, the planning and execution of the plan should be done by January 1 of the junior year. The financial information from the junior year will be reported on the first financial aid application forms in the senior year.

The college night presentation that I just commented on was not an exception: all of the college night presentations I've attended have contained incorrect information. The main reason I chose to write about this particular presentation was because of the abundance of specific information that was provided. I discourage parents from relying on information provided at college night to make decisions about college selection or financial aid. I have never found the quality of information at college nights to be satisfying. In each instance, the guest speaker was a college financial aid officer. The information was biased towards the type of institution where the speaker worked. When the speakers came from a public college, little information about private colleges was provided, and vice versa. On top of that, an abundance of the information from the so-called experts was completely wrong.

POINTS TO REMEMBER

Chapter 7

False Information from Surprising Sources

- College night presentations often come too late for parents to reallocate assets in preparation for filling in the FAFSA and CSS Profile. Ideally, any assets should be reallocated by the end of the student's sophomore year. The financial information from the junior year will be reported on the FAFSA in the student's senior year.

- Parents might expect college night to offer a broad overview of college admissions and financial aid. However, the presenter usually provides more information about public colleges or private colleges, depending on the type of college where the speaker works.

- Speakers at college night are often poorly informed about the details of FAFSA. At each college night that I have attended, the speaker has provided incorrect information.

- High schools often invite a college financial aid officer to speak at college night. College financial aid officers can help the family understand the college's financial aid application policies and procedures, and informs you of scholarship opportunities. However, you should not rely on a college financial aid officer to give you advice about college choices, help you reallocate assets to reduce the Expected Family Contribution, or make plans to pay for college in the most tax-advantaged way.

- An experienced college financial aid consultant can help you to:

    1) *Choose colleges that fit your needs and budget.*

    2) *Do a pre-planning analysis of your family's goals and financial situation and allocate your assets to maximize financial aid.*

    3) *Fill in all financial aid forms consistently and correctly.*

    4) *Negotiate for a better financial aid package when it's appropriate.*

    5) *Make a personal how-to-pay plan that covers college costs in the most tax-favored way for all of your children.*

Steps to Take Control

Find an experienced college financial aid consultant. An experienced financial aid consultant should be able to answer the following questions in a satisfactory way. Examples of satisfactory answers are provided.

1) *How can you help me choose colleges that fit my needs and budget?*

Answer: I would find out what your student is interested in studying and review your assets. We would look for colleges that have strong programs in your student's field of interest. At the same time, we would look for colleges that tend to give students like yours good financial aid. [Read Chapter 2 for a more thorough description of the process that I follow]

2) *What is the most common way of reducing the Expected Family Contribution?*

Answer: The most common way is to reposition assets from reportable accounts to non-reportable accounts. [For your information: It is not always beneficial for a family to do this. For more information, read Chapter 3.]

3) *How would you help me submit my financial aid forms correctly and on time?*

Answer: We would make financial estimates and enter them consistently on all financial aid applications. As soon as you are finished with your federal tax forms, we would submit revisions to the applications. [Chapter 4 provides a more detailed description of this process.]

4) *When is it appropriate to negotiate for a better financial aid package? How would you do it?*

Answer: It's appropriate to appeal for better financial aid when the college of your choice has made an offer that is low for a student like yours. The best way to appeal is to provide documents to make the college aware of the shortfall in their package. [Chapter 5 contains further advice regarding negotiations.]

5) *What would you do to help me determine the best way to pay for college?*

Answer: I would review your assets and consider your financial goals. We would look for a way that would provide the best financial aid and the maximum tax advantage. [More details are provided in Chapter 6.]

Dear Reader,

By now, I hope you understand how to take control of the college financial aid process. Let me remind you of the five key steps:

1) **Pick colleges that will give your student the best financial packages.**

2) **Do a financial pre-planning to increase your eligibility for FREE money.**

3) **Fill in all the financial aid forms correctly.**

4) **Negotiate for a better financial aid package when it's appropriate.**

5) **Pay for college on a tax-favored basis.**

Sorting through the options and making choices can seem overwhelming. However, proper planning can put your family in a better financial situation after the college years. Planning will also let you rest assured that you can pay for an education at a college that will help your student reach his/her goals.

I love working with families through the college financial aid process. Many families come to me full of fear and anxiety. As we go through the process together, I help families consider their options and help them make clear decisions. In the end, families feel more strong and confident because they have found a path to pay for an affordable college that meets the student's expectations.

I encourage you to contact my office for a free consultation. During the consultation, I like to get a general idea of the student's educational goals as well as the family's financial goals and situation. Every family's needs are different. Some families appreciate finding a way to pay for college on a tax-favored basis most of all. Others benefit most by making the right college picks. Some families need help negotiating for the financial assistance that they deserve. During that first visit, I will listen to your family's situation and let you know how I could help you through the college financial aid process. At that point, it is up to you and your family to go home and decide whether you would like me to help you with your admissions and financial aid plan.

I welcome the opportunity!

Kevin Simme

For More Information

Visit us at **www.kevinsimme.com**
for news, updates, and more.

Send questions/comments to: **info@kevinsimme.com**

Call **(609) 799-2500** to make an appointment.

About the Authors

Kevin Simme is the president and founder of College Funding Alternatives, which he started in 1997 as a safe haven for those seeking assistance through the process of college admissions and financial aid. Kevin helps families approach the process with other priorities in mind, such as saving for retirement or paying for the care of elderly parents. Furthermore, he helps students gain admission to affordable college programs that let them realize their dreams and aspirations. With his guidance, family members work together to make decisions and take control of what might have seemed like an overwhelming process. Kevin attended Houghton College where he received his BA degree in 1985. After college, he joined MarketSource Corporation, a college marketing and event planning company that worked with major corporations to reach college students on campuses across the USA and Canada. His work gave him a unique perspective on the importance of college environment to a successful college experience. His wide knowledge of college programs makes it easy for him to help students match their aspirations with college choices.

With a balanced approach to working with families, this husband and father of three is prepared to help you discover The Key To Paying For College so you can Unlock Secrets That Could Save You Thousands!

David Anderson is an educator and writer. He earned a BA in English from Cornell University and a MA in Linguistics from the University of Pittsburgh without incurring any debt. As an educator, he has taught students to express themselves in English in a variety of contexts from junior high and high schools to college-level and adult education programs. As an author, he has written two other works that were published by Longman.

David lives with his wife and four children in New Jersey. His oldest son is working and his daughter is completing a BS degree and preparing to attend medical school. He has two younger sons who look forward to attending college as well.